WHALE TALES

Human Interactions With Whales
volume two

Pita Fromm

Whale Tales Press • Friday Harbor, Washington USA

Whale Tales Press
PO Box 865 • Friday Harbor, Washington 98250
360/378-8378

Front cover photo ©1992 Eric Martin - See story on page 29

Back cover photo ©1993 Terry Domico- See story on page 42

Photo of Jim Nollman by Betty Didcoct ©1994 Interspecies Communication

Bernard Moitessier, translated by William Rodarmor, THE LONG WAY.
Dobbs Ferry, NY: Sheridan House, Inc. 1973, 1995

Whale Tales was designed and laid out by:
Bruce Conway • Friday Harbor, Washington 98250
Edited by Andrew Seltser

For ordering information,
please call Whale Tales Press at: **1-800-669-3950**
Quantity purchase discounts are available.

Please contact Peter J. Fromm through Whale Tales Press to schedule
speaking/reading engagements or multimedia presentations.

Library of Congress Cataloging-in Publication Data
Fromm, Peter J. (1947 -   )
        Whale Tales: Human Interactions With Whales, volume
        two/ Collected By Peter J. Fromm

        ISBN 0-9648704-1-X

        1. Whales   2. Whale—World   3. Folktales—Whales   4. Interspecies
        Communication   II. Title
        LOCCC# 95-90817

Manufactured in the United States of America.

Dedication

For people protecting and healing our environment:
may many others join you soon - keep the faith.

Whale Tales
Human Interactions With Whales

Introduction

Orca Tales

Minke Tales

Humpback Tales

Gray Whale Tales

Dolphin Tales

Whales Come to Boats

Surfing With Whales

Flotsam

Research

Communication

Death and Dying

Rescues

Transformation & Metaphysics

Epilogue

Appendices

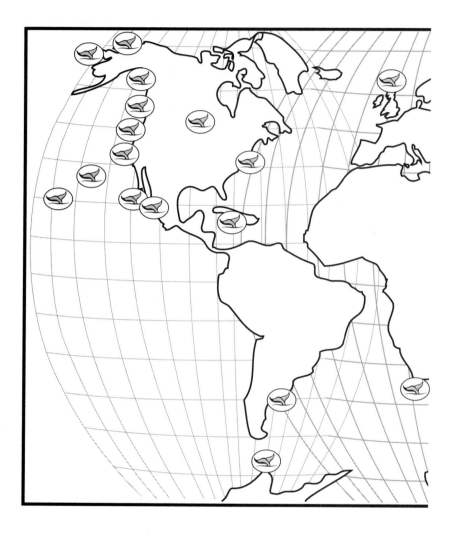

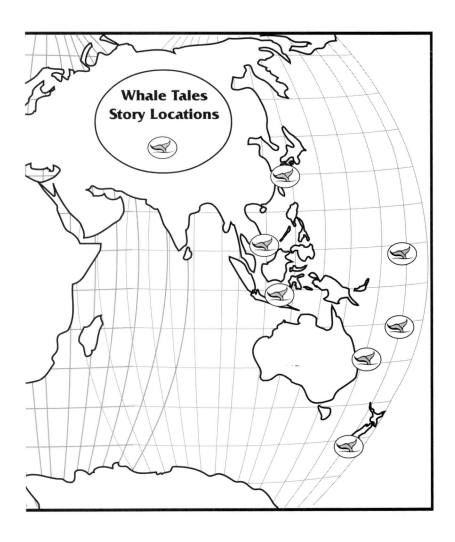

Whale Tales
Story Locations

Introduction

Affirmation

Mary Wondra and her husband Glen Coye live and work at a 1,400 acre forest preserve Unitarian Retreat and Conference Center in western Massachusetts. They are part of a community of eight people who are responsible for maintaining the facility and providing the infrastructure for the programs that are taught there.

In January 1997, my husband Glen and I were in Hawaii when a global meditation for peace took place. The idea was that people around the world, all at the same time, would pay some attention to simply thinking about world peace. It seemed like a good idea to us. A group from the retreat center where we were staying walked down to a point of land on the Pacific Ocean. It was a beautiful spot with waves crashing against black lava rocks, coconut palms that had been planted over the past ten years, and young palms sprouting from coconuts, growing in grass among the rocks.

We gathered before sunrise, sat there on the grass and lava and centered ourselves being silent and breathing deeply. Fifteen minutes later, when it was 'the time' for the global meditation, a group of humpback whales with a flotilla of dolphins swam by about two hundred yards off shore. They simply swam past us from left to right for fifteen minutes, at the very moment we were all focused on being part of this global meditation, thinking about peace on Earth. It really felt like an affirmation.

Maybe there was some energy among those cetaceans that was also contributing to what we were thinking and feeling.

Commitment

Captain Paul Watson is the Founder and International President of the Sea Shepherd Conservation Society. He also teaches ecology at UCLA and Pasadena College of Design.

I regret that my whale tale is of a different and much darker nature than most of the stories of contact between humans and whales related in this book. But while it is violent and bloody, it is also of a piece with the recollections you will read herein because, as has been true for so many others, the moment when I met a whale was awe-inspiring and deeply moving, and it changed my life.

In June 1975, I was the First Mate on board the Greenpeace V when we encountered the Soviet whaling fleet sixty miles off the coast of Northern California. We were there to intervene against the killing of whales, and it was my job to pilot the lead 'kamikaze' inflatable in a tactic where we would place our bodies directly between the harpoon gun and the defenseless whales. We were reading quite a bit of Gandhi at the time, and naively believed the whalers would not risk killing a human being in their quest to kill whales. We were wrong.

Robert Hunter, one of the founders of Greenpeace, and I found ourselves in a small boat racing over heavy swells. Bearing down behind us was a huge kill boat, and despite her grim rust-besmeared hull, she was cutting through the sea at twenty knots. Directly before us were eight magnificent sperm whales, fleeing for their lives. Their breath was exploding in frantic panic. They were unable to inhale enough life-giving oxygen to dive and seek the safety of the depths. We could smell the fear in the mist of their exhalations, and marveled at the smooth beauty of their powerful bodies.

Robert and I turned to face each other. I had my hand on the throttle and he clung to the safety line in the bow. We were doing what we came to do, and it was an historical moment. Never before had human beings used their own bodies as shields to protect whales. Damn we felt good, and we felt confident our actions would save them.

Behind us on the bow of the whaler, the Russian harpooner crouched and waggled his big cannon about, looking for a shot. I followed the blunt point of the four-foot grenade-tipped projectile and maneuvered to always keep ourselves in his line of sight. The harpooner was becoming increasingly frustrated.

For twenty glorious, exhilarating minutes we blocked his shot. Finally the captain, a big brute of a man, strode like a maddened gladiator down the catwalk of the whaler and approached the exasperated harpooner. He yelled into the man's ear, and then turned, looked down on us, smiled evilly, and menacingly brought his finger across his throat.

A few minutes later, the ship's massive prow rose up on a swell as our little boat descended into a trough. Ahead, atop another swell, the eight whales rose into the line of fire. A thunderous boom shook us as the harpoon sliced over our heads and slammed into the backside of a female, the cable slashing the water only a few feet from us. Amidst a shower of blood and flesh, her pitiful scream assaulted our ears.

We were stunned. We watched helplessly as blood enshrouded the dark blue sea. The largest whale in the pod suddenly swam away from the others. His body broke the surface as he dove, his tail lifted out of the water before disappearing.

We had been warned by the experts that a bull would turn and defend his pod. Robert and I had both read *Moby Dick* and had seen old woodcuts of enraged wounded sperm whales breaking whale boats like match sticks, hurling New England whalers to their watery grave.

Thus it was, stomachs churning with anxiety, as we waited apprehensively for sixty tons of fear and rage to come rocketing up beneath us. The dying female was still churning the sea into froth, whimpering now, her spout misting the air with pink droplets. The ship had stopped, the harpooner was loading a new missile, but not having time to attach it to a cable before jumping back behind the sights, his finger nonchalantly stroking the trigger.

Suddenly the sea erupted. The whale's mighty square head broke the surface behind us. His body arched up, his eyes focused on the man crouching behind the gun. The cannon roared a second time as a harpoon fired at point blank range exploded inside the spermaceti-filled chamber of the whale's head. He screamed in agony as the metal shrapnel shred his sensitive flesh. The whale fell back, blood splashing obscenely into the sea, his body convulsing before the unmerciful twentieth century killing machine.

The whale's head slowly emerged from the water angling over us. His body rose upwards until his eye was at the same height as mine. The water and the blood from his wound fell upon us like rain. Rivulets of coagulated blood and brine slithered like scarlet worms over the boat's pontoons and our wet suits. As I looked into his eye I knew instantly the whale was aware of our futile effort to save him and his pod.

At that moment, the whale could have chosen to kill us. His body merely had to drop to crush us. He could have easily seized us and the boat in his mighty jaws. His six-foot jaw hung open and his six-inch teeth were so close I could have reached out and wrapped my hand around one of them.

But he did not harm us. He hovered there, his eye the size of my fist peering deep into my own. I saw my reflection in his eye, and sensed that he knew we were not his enemy. I was struck by another feeling as I saw pity in that dying whale. It was not a pity for himself, or for his kind, but for us.

The primary product the Russians were extracting from these slain giants was a high-grade heat resistant organic oil to be used for lubricating ICBM missiles. They were destroying the whales to manufacture a horrific weapon meant to incinerate human beings. The thought struck me like a revelation that my species was absolutely insane.

The whale slowly and deliberately sank back into the water. I watched his eye slide sadly beneath the surface, his life flickering to an untimely end. He sank out of sight, then turned and came to the surface once more, his body twitching momentarily before being stilled forever, softly undulating upon the surface with a widening pool of scarlet blood spreading and befouling the blue of the Pacific.

Because the harpooner had not fastened a cable onto his death-dealing weapon, the whale was not attached to the ship and sank to the bottom. His murder was a total waste.

I was angry, intensely angry. On that day I turned my back on humanity and became a proud traitor to my species. That whale could have slain us, yet chose to spare us. How could such a debt be repaid?

I left Greenpeace to establish the Sea Shepherd Conservation Society. This has given me the freedom to take an aggressive stand against the enemies of whalekind.

Since that day twenty-five years ago, I have done my best to repay that wondrous creature. In his name we have scuttled and destroyed nine whaling ships, and shut down whaling operations worldwide.

In November 1986, a few days after we sank half of the Icelandic whaling fleet, I was confronted by a former colleague from Greenpeace. He walked up to me and angrily said, "What you did in Iceland is criminal, unforgivable, and despicable."

I looked at him and answered, "So?"

He was taken aback and said, "What gives you the right to attack the property of others, to set yourself up as judge and jury? I think you should be ashamed of yourself."

I told him, "You know, I really don't care what you or any other human being thinks about it. We didn't sink those ships for you. We sank them for the whales, and if you can find a single whale that disagrees with what we did, then we will reconsider our tactics."

Looking into that whale's eye a quarter of a century ago set me on a path and gave me a purpose that I still pursue. It is my dream, my quest, and my crusade to stop the worldwide slaughter of whales and dolphins. Perhaps it is unobtainable; perhaps it is unrealistic, considering the continuing psychotic behavior of humankind towards the non-human world. Perhaps it is indeed folly. But I cannot do anything else. His eye haunts me still, and my debt remains unpaid.

On that day so long ago, a whale taught me to view the world from another perspective - from his perspective. It is both my curse and my joy to fight for whalekind against the cruelty and arrogance of humankind. I will not live in a world without whales, and I will not stand by and watch them be driven into oblivion without lifting a finger to stop the killing.

The only use a whaling ship has to me is as an underwater habitat for fish. I have no use for whalers, and no sympathy for their brutish and barbaric livelihoods. The whaler is a scum encrusted blemish upon the escutcheon of humankind, and his cruel anachronistic trade should go the way of the slaver, the torturer, and the child pornographer. Whaling should be abolished and made a crime against life and beauty.

In saving the whale, we are regaining our sanity, our decency and our sensitivity. We save them not just for their sake, but also for the sake of our very survival. If we cannot save the whales, we will not be able to save our seas. If the sea and its myriad diversity of life is lost, the end will be in sight for the survival of humankind. All that we are, the good and the bad, will be gone forever.

From the Author

In the spring of 1998, a fellow whale watching boat Captain told me *Taku* - K 1 - was missing and presumed dead. How sad.

Taku was the easiest whale to identify. Two notches were cut into his dorsal fin in the early seventies as part of the first census of the southern resident killer whales. At that time, marine parks were capturing and killing sixty-eight whales. Most of these were young animals who would be in the prime of their breeding lives if they were still alive. The captors claimed hundreds of orcas lived in these waters. In fact, when researchers counted them, seventy-five killer whales were identified.

Over years of taking people out to see whales, I had observed *Taku* many times, and made quite a few photographs of him. Several of the pictures show *Taku* swimming close to his mother, *Lummi*.

Throughout the day I learned of *Taku's* death, my thoughts returned to him: visualizing the photos, recalling the encounters, and hearing the whale tales people shared about their interactions with *Taku*. Everything dies, and mourning is alright.

I went out to spend the night in my twenty-four foot dugout canoe, savoring nature. I slept in the boat under the stars. Eagles' calls woke me. An osprey caught a fish near my anchored boat. Kingfishers flew around squealing. River otters climbed out of the water to spend some time ashore. Just what I needed after weeks of intense boat repairs.

As I motored out of the bay, orcas' dorsal fins caught my attention. They were heading my way! I shut down and drifted as about fifteen whales swam by. One female surfaced four times within twenty feet of the canoe, and a strong feeling of peace and joy, with sadness too, came over me. I was able to memorize the nicks on her fin and her saddle patch. They looked familiar but I did not know just which whale she was.

I stayed with them for thirty minutes then returned to Friday Harbor, wondering about that female orca, and the sensation I experienced. In my office I looked at the photos of *Taku*. Sure enough, that whale was *Lummi*, his mom. I felt her saying, "Yes, *Taku* is gone. Thanks for thinking of him."

And on another tack, whales were in the news again the other day.

Great news: the Mitsubishi corporation abandoned their plan to build a huge salt evaporating complex in San Ignacio Lagoon. And, *Keiko*, the *Free Willy* whale, was given more swimming room again.

Not so long ago, few people cared about the construction of a salt plant in a gray whale calving lagoon, or about a captive whale's plight. Today they do.

Humans all over the planet are experiencing interactions with whales. Through education about cetaceans via television, books, magazines, and news stories, vast numbers of people are becoming aware that there is some powerful, historic, and undefinable connection between our species. This is the tip of the iceberg of recognizing our true relationship with nature.

I wish we two-legged creatures would clearly act as if the value of other animals, and plants - and our dependence on nature - was important. Everything in our lives, with the exception of meteorites and moon rocks, comes from the natural resources of the Earth. Our self-centered view that the human role is to dominate nature must change if our children's children are going to live in a healthy world. When you look through a year's worth of *National Geographic* magazines, it is evident on every continent that habitat necessary for animals and plants to live, feed, and reproduce is disappearing.

I hope the stories in this volume of *Whale Tales* will move you to look at the needs of nature. Dramatic changes in many humans' lives have happened because of their interactions with cetaceans. Equally dramatic changes must take place in human behavior and life styles if frogs and fish, cheetahs and gorillas, eagles and swans, salmon and trout, ferns and redwoods will be here in the future. These are not new words or thoughts. April 2000 marked the thirtieth anniversary of Earth Day, and what, really, has changed in the way humans live on this good Earth in those three decades?

Many Whale Tales are great examples of joy, love, hope, perseverance, faith, and magic. Perhaps a change in consciousness or paradigm shift will actually happen and everything will be better: the pollution we have created will disappear, the population will dramatically shrink without massive trauma, peace will prevail. Here's hoping, working, and living toward that end.

Peter J. Fromm
Friday Harbor, Washington
April, 2000

*"The significant problems we face
cannot be solved
at the same level of thinking
that created them."*

Albert Einstein

Orca Tales

Whatcha Doin?

Jim Justice decided that he did not want to be a surgeon any longer, so he went back to Johns Hopkins University to get a degree in epidemiology and preventive medicine. Jim asked for an assignment from the Indian Health Service to do a special job in southeast Alaska, where he worked with the Tlingit people organizing health councils and a prepaid health network where each village would have its own health program. Jim boated around and got to know a lot of the area.

While working in Alaska, my schedule did not always allow me to travel with other people, I got my own boat. She was a beautiful red cedar boat, *Erna*, built by a Norwegian who lived on her at Sitka for many years. She was a little trawler with both an inboard and an outboard motor.

I was going through the Inland Passage on a rare, cloudless day, fishing for king salmon. All of a sudden, my trolling motor stopped. I put the inboard motor on, tied the wheel to hold course, and stepped onto the swim step at the stern looking for the reason why the outboard motor quit. It was tangled up with something that looked like an old piece of net. I tilted the motor up and leaned out and tried to get this stuff off the propellor.

All of a sudden a shadow passed over me. I was startled. I turned around to look out, away from the boat. I did not see anything but a glistening black piece of slate, like a blackboard. What I was looking at kept moving, and I recognized it as the dorsal fin of a male killer whale that had come within arm's length of me! I realized that he must have come up to get a good look at me untangling the propellor.

I could have touched the whale, he had been that close. I thought it was unusual. I had not heard of anyone getting that close to a killer whale. (This was 1963.) Other people had sighted killer whales at a distance, but the whales took off when boats got within fifty yards.

I had no idea that a killer whale would ever come so close to a person, and I wondered if he was trolling for humans. That was an eye opener. It scared the daylights out of me. I was shaking so badly I gave up trying to get the prop cleared on the outboard, went into the cabin and motored back home with the inboard. I had no reason to be frightened. I had never heard a single tale of anyone ever being harmed by a killer whale. ◄

Where's My Fish???

Debbie Bledsoe moved to the San Juan Islands in 1985. She is very active with the efforts to free Lolita, a captive orca in Miami, Florida. Debbie has taken many friends out to see the whales, including Olivia Newton John who came to the San Juan Islands with her Australian film crew, Wildlife, to record the orca whales.

Several years ago, after the end of the whale watching season in the San Juan Islands, I was out boating with a friend. It was one of those rare November days which was beautifully sunny, still and inviting. We had packed a picnic lunch. We planned to drop a couple of hooks and troll around Open Bay to enjoy what might have been the last sunny day before winter. It was the middle of the week, and there were no other boats out.

Usually there are no orcas in the area so late in the year, but while we were fishing we saw fins going by. They were out in Haro Strait about halfway to Vancouver Island, heading south. The orcas were spread widely apart, foraging for food. We decided to pull in our fishing gear and get closer to the whales to say good-bye to them for the year. We were going at the boat's top speed, about ten knots, rumbling slowly along towards where we had sighted the whales. My friend Van saw a whale close to the boat. I turned off the motor and we sat there rocking in our own wake.

All of a sudden, a huge fin came out of the water by our starboard side. A male orca was swimming on the surface towards us. He was *Taku*, K 1, the easiest whale to identify because of two notches in his dorsal fin. He stayed right there as if we had interrupted him. I stood at the back of the boat apologizing to the whale for cutting him off.

Van and I were standing by the transom and *Taku* was still on the surface within twenty feet of the boat. We were in the middle of Haro Strait, ours was the only boat on the water. *Taku* came up parallel to the side of the twenty-seven foot boat. He was much longer. His dorsal fin was above my eye level. I began to get excited because, not only was I getting to say good-bye to the whales, I was also having a close encounter.

Taku circled the boat, then came to the stern. He dove under the swim step, and must have turned around beneath us because he came

Orca Tales   3

Taku   *Photo: Peter Fromm*

out head first under the swim step going away from us. Van said she was getting scared, and wanted me to start the motor. I told her we were too close to *Taku*, who had begun making side passes and going under and around the boat. We were the focus of his attention for fifteen minutes. I looked over the side and suddenly saw a very tired twenty-pound salmon hiding under the swim step of my boat. I figured out what was going on: *Taku* was chasing the salmon, and the fish was using the bottom of the boat as a hiding place.

Being a fisherperson, I reached over and caught the salmon in my net. Then I realized this was *Taku's* fish, so I dumped the salmon back into the water. With renewed energy, the salmon swam off. The next thing I knew, *Taku* came up in a spyhop, five feet off the port side of the transom where I was standing, and several feet above us. *Taku* held himself in that position longer than any spyhop I had ever seen. He leaned in towards the boat. I was standing there, eye to eye with *Taku*. He scanned over the back of the boat looking for his fish!

Watching the whale's eye was mesmerizing. I began to back away from the side of the boat and the whale. I began to feel afraid. My heart was beating fast. Van had jumped below into the cabin and was yelling at me to get us out of there. *Taku* looked at me again. I told him I didn't have his fish. I could not believe I had thrown it back. I would have loved to have handed it to the whale. *Taku* went back down into the water. Again Van yelled at me to turn on the motor.

Taku came back up again in a spyhop and looked into the boat from the other side. Van was watching out of the window from the cabin. She saw the fish hiding under her side of the boat and ran out onto the deck. Van pointed at the salmon and screamed, "Your fish is right here! Your fish is right here!" *Taku* submerged and swam around. He came up and made a little splash with his tail, then he swam off. We never saw the fish again, so I presume he got it.

We were so stunned that we floated for miles after *Taku* left us. We were south of Victoria, out in Juan de Fuca Strait, before I started the motor. We spent all that time trying to understand and digest what had happened. 🐋

Have More Fish!

__Kevin Monahan__ was born in England, and has worked on the water since 1975. He was a fisherman for twelve years. He has worked for the Canadian Coast Guard since 1990, both as Captain of a patrol boat and in fisheries enforcement.

In 1986, just off the mouth of the Fraser River, I was gill netting for salmon as deck hand on a thirty-eight foot boat. The water's surface was like glass. The visibility was extremely limited. Gray sky, gray water. It was not exactly foggy, just misty with very low clouds. There was no distinction between the sea and the sky. We were floating in a gray liquid world. The only thing that indicated to us that we were not actually floating in space was the line of corks holding up the net going off the stern, and the occasional piece of seaweed drifting by on the surface. It was very calm and very beautiful.

We started to hear blows. We had a pretty good idea what was in the vicinity and what that sound meant: killer whale, probably frightening all the fish in the area away. We were a little concerned. We had not had great success catching salmon. This was the major part of our season, fishing right off the Fraser River for sockeye. We were aware that a killer whale in the area might seriously affect our catch.

I looked up and in the distance I could see a disturbance on the water through the mist. Sure enough, it was a big bull killer whale. His dorsal fin stood up in the mist like a paddle from a native canoe. As we had feared, he was swimming down the inside curve of our net, the side the fish were approaching from.

As the whale came closer, we could see that instead of scaring the fish away from the net, he was scaring them into the net! Each time a fish got caught, the corkline would be momentarily tugged underwater. In his wake, the corks of our net were bouncing and bumping up and down.

I was sure he was getting his fair share of fish. The whale continued swimming along the entire length of our net, very slowly surfacing and diving again, barely submerging his dorsal fin each time. As he approached the boat we could see more clearly how the net behind him was shaking and jumping. We realized that instead of being a bad guy, this killer whale was our friend. He was doing us a big favor! The whale was about thirty feet off the net and continued swimming towards the boat. Just before he reached the side of the boat he dove. He was so close that I could have reached out and touched his dorsal fin with my hand. We ran to the other side of the boat, expecting to see the dorsal fin come up, and the whale to continue on his way, ignoring us. Instead, he rose up, spyhopped, and exposed his head. The whale was five to ten feet from the side of the boat. He stared at us for what seemed like a minute - then he blew.

Anybody that has smelled whale breath will know that it is not a pleasant experience. As far as we were concerned though, it was well worth it that day.

There were a lot of fish in our net, and we spoke only praise of killer whales after that.

No Fear

Roberto Bubas has been a Park Ranger at the Peninsula Valdes National Park in Argentina since 1992. The park has right whales, elephant seals, sea lions and killer whales. Roberto studied marine biology in university.

My main interest is the killer whales. I have a project which began in 1993 taking ID photos of them. There are no more than twenty of these whales in the area around Peninsula Valdes National Park.

Roberto Bubas and killer whale   *Photo: unknown*

The killer whales here have an impressive feeding behavior to catch sea lion and elephant seal pups right off the beach. There is an inlet on the Peninsula where, when the tide begins to go up, the whales enter to catch pups.

Two years ago I waited there and when the killer whales were entering the inlet, I went into the water. I was sitting there and began making sounds, splashing and blowing bubbles with my face in the water. Two female killer whales came in close to me. They were logging at the surface, two meters away.

After that encounter, the whales came to find me in the same place several times. I got deeper into the water and they swam closer, almost touching me. When I played my harmonica for them, they rolled over each other to get closer to me.

I was also in the water with *Mel,* a big male who was maybe thirty five years old. He had a brother, *Bernardo.* Perhaps you know them, because in all of the movies about killer whales in Patagonia, these brothers are the stars. *(Note: National Geographic's* Wolves of the

Roberto Bubas and friend

Sea *is one such movie – pjf)* Unfortunately, *Bernardo* died three years ago and *Mel*, hunting alone now, has had less success in his attacks. They often hunted together as a team, and the pups did not realize there were two whales after them. Sea lions and elephant seals are also intelligent. When adults see the orca's dorsal fins, they know there is danger for them. They learn this as pups.

We believed *Mel* was not well-fed, as he had to do more work and harder work as a single hunter. It is very unusual to see only one orca chasing the pups - almost all of them hunt in pairs.

I felt this would be a good time to prove that *Mel* wouldn't hurt me. We had witnessed him miss two pups in his attacks. So perhaps he was angry as well as hungry. I went to the beach, got into the water and began to make bubbling sounds with my mouth and hands. The killer whales are able to catch animals in very shallow water so *Mel* could have caught me easily, as I was in up to my waist.

I captured his attention. *Mel* stopped, turned and swam towards me. He began to swim very fast, right at me. When *Mel* was two feet away, he veered and went back out into deeper waters. I could not feel his echo location clicks on me, but I believe he was using that sense. I was a little afraid and nervous. When you have a big whale swimming very fast towards you, and you know what happens with the three ton elephant seals, you have some fear. I cannot remember what I felt at that moment, except that I had to have a lot of courage to stay in the water without moving and wait to see what happened.

My friends on the shore who were taking pictures and watching the whale swim towards me, breaking the seas as he came, were yelling, "Roberto! Come Out!" There were other people witnessing me in the water with *Mel*. They thought I was crazy.

I stayed there. It was very impressive to see the whale searching, then finding me and Zooommm! like a torpedo towards me. I felt afraid, but I could stay in the water because I believed that the whale would not hurt me.

Even though I knew Mel wouldn't hurt me, it was a powerful image in my mind having watched this animal successfully hunt elephant seals and sea lions many times. I knew that he could catch me without any problems. It was crazy, but I was sure that Mel would not hurt me. I was crying when I came back to the shore and my friends.

Killer whales are intelligent animals with very strong personalities like humans, and can sometimes be angry or playful. But I have never feared them.

I believe they are magical, special beings. My treasure is keeping this friendship with them. This is my life. I do not want anything other than to enjoy my killer whale friends at the edge of the beach. 🐋

Take That

Bruce Conway is the Macintosh guru in the San Juan Islands. He also designs and lays out books for self-publishing authors and artists.

My friend Diane and I were at South Beach on San Juan Island. She had come for a visit and we decided to go for a walk in the afternoon. We saw part of one of the resident pods of orcas swim by fairly close to the shore. There were six to eight of them. We noticed an aluminium skiff full of fishermen pursuing the whales. The guys in the boat were speeding right up to the whales from behind when they surfaced, stopping close in front of them, and generally harassing this small family group. There were no other boats around.

We saw the large male in the pod drop back about one hundred yards behind the others. He began to swim very fast, right on the surface, directly towards the boat. He sounded, then made a full breach. The whale made a perfect cannonball, maybe fifteen feet from the boat, with deliberate aim. He generated such a huge, well-directed wave that it washed all four of the men out into the open water. I have never heard screams so loud in my life! In a heartbeat, these macho guys went from cockiness to thinking they might be eaten.

The orca let them be. He had done his job protecting his family and moved on. Diane had never seen orcas before and was thoroughly impressed. I had seen whales many times, but was also amazed by this behavior. It took the fishermen quite a while, but they all climbed back into the boat. They were thoroughly subdued. Cold water and orca intimidation shriveled many things including their egos. ✍

Nature Does You

'Spike' Kane *was born in Liverpool, England. He was a bicycle messenger in London until he moved to Orcas Island, Washington. He spent two summers teaching kayaking, canoeing and sailing at YMCA Camp Orkila, then started his own kayak business on Lopez Island. He moved to Seattle to study wooden boat building. He now repairs boats.*

Early in the summer, I took a couple from Maryland on a kayak trip in Juan de Fuca Strait. They were impeccably dressed, as if they were ready for a day on the terraces watching cricket. She had a big, flamboyant hat and a nice matching top and skirt. He was wearing white linen pants and shirt. The people were excited. They asked if they would see whales. I told them there was always a chance. Sometimes we saw whales, but on most trips we did not.

Because it was so calm, I decided to do the trip from the south end of the island. It was very exposed, often rough open water. There are not a lot of opportunities to paddle in Juan de Fuca Strait. On this day, the Strait was like a pond. You could clearly see the Olympic Mountains, twenty miles away, reflected in the water. There was not a breath of wind.

I spent about thirty minutes on land going over kayak safety. I was about to push their kayak into the water when the woman asked her husband to get the camera. He asked me if they would need it. I told them there was always a possibility that we might see something out there. "Well, have you ever actually seen any whales out there?" he asked with a bit of sarcasm. I told him I hadn't. So he says, brusquely,

"All right, then. Let's just go." So off we went. As we were paddling away, I thought to myself that this was probably going to be the one day something would happen, and none of us had a camera.

We paddled the mile from MacKay Harbor to Iceberg Point the couple was getting used to the kayak. All of us were enjoying the beautiful weather. We paddled around Iceberg Point staying close to the shore which went in a straight line to a tiny point. This was followed by a shallow cove with high cliff-like walls. There were thick kelp beds all along the way. We stopped in the cove, popped off our spray skirts and relaxed. There was a gentle lapping of water against the bottom of the cliff, and no signs of humans in view.

I kept about fifty feet away from the couple, giving them a chance to be on their own. We had been there five minutes when I heard them discussing something, or perhaps arguing. I asked if everything was alright, and the man hesitantly said, "Well...she thinks she's seen a whale." I asked, "Oh really? Where?"

I expected them to point out into the Strait, but she pointed in the water between me and them and said, "It just popped its head up and went back down."

I never knew of whales being seen in this cove; we were too close to shore, the water was not deep enough. The surface was still. She said it looked like a dolphin. She sounded as if she did not believe it herself at this time.

Suddenly, there was a loud, 'Kchooooowwwfff' at the back of their kayak. An adult male orca rolled to the surface and sprayed all over them. His fin did a cartwheel two feet away from their kayak as it went down into the water. I said, "Ah-ha! Now that is a whale!"

Whales surfaced all around us in the cove. A super pod, all three southern resident pods, close to one hundred whales were coming round the point into the cove by us and out again into Juan de Fuca Strait. As soon as I saw these whales appear, I knew we had to get out of there. I started paddling in line with the whales, telling the couple not to worry.

She was visibly shaken. He was now very awkward in his movements. Their eyes were huge with a mixture of fear and amazement. The whales were coming straight toward them. They said in unison, "Oh My God!"

Their boat was perpendicular to the direction the whales were swimming. I told them to turn their kayak parallel with the whales. All the man wanted to do was paddle backwards towards the cliffs. He could not think, so I continued to coach him. "Push down with your right foot, paddle forward and the boat will turn."

As I was saying this, another dorsal fin was heading straight for the center of their kayak. It was waving as it came towards them higher than their heads. It was the biggest fin of them all. The man was frozen, his paddle stopped in mid-stroke. The couple put their paddles on the deck of the kayak and stared up at the whale's fin. Their jaws dropped and their mouths opened wide as if they wanted to scream in terror, but they were silent. The fin started to descend as it came nearer. It missed the kayak by inches. The couple turned their heads in unison, watching as the whale swam underneath them and came up on the other side.

I told them they were okay, and to follow the way I was paddling. At last they managed to paddle out of the cove. The whales continued to come slowly towards us. As we got to the point of the cove, two baby whales swam next to us, spiraling around each other. I heard their vocalizations resonating through the kayak's hull. I yelled to the couple to listen inside their boat, but I had lost them. They were just strangely dressed, out of place people in a boat, wishing they were any place but in a kayak surrounded by orcas.

By now I was euphoric, paddling after the two young whales. I had forgotten everything I knew about kayaking around these animals.

They calves were very close to my kayak, taking turns surfacing and spiraling. Unwittingly I got between them and a female, maybe the mom. She breached right between my kayak and the two calves. She came out of the water just at the end of my paddle. She went straight up into the air and turned. Her beautiful white belly looked like a hard boiled egg. It was the cleanest thing I had ever seen. In midair, she turned and dropped with a huge splash next to the bow of my kayak. I stopped paddling and the bow of the boat rose up into the wall of water her splash created. Suddenly it all came back to me: do not paddle near the whales.

What we had seen was only the beginning of the super pod. The whales kept coming. For twenty minutes they swam past us, a whale surfacing every five to twenty seconds never further than fifty feet from us. We sat in our little boats, off the tiny cove, as they swam to Iceberg Point and towards the west side of San Juan Island. We watched them disappear.

As we paddled back, I excitedly told the couple how fantastic that encounter was. They mumbled a few times, but were mostly silent.

We got back to the beach and said our good-byes, and they drove to the B & B. Later, the owner of the B & B told me the couple had collapsed like rag dolls into easy chairs and stared out into Swift's Bay. They appeared to be in shock. He greeted them warmly and asked how their trip was.

They were stone-faced and silent. They looked at each other, then the man swallowed and slowly said, "Well, you see, we are from the East Coast. We don't 'do' nature." And with that, they told the story of what they had experienced. ⌐≺

Tuggy Sees the Whales

*Tuggy the cat lived with **Peter Fromm** aboard* Uwila *for ten and one half of his eleven years. Peter is presently writing a book about the adventures of Tuggy the sailing cat.*

In January 1993, we were sailing back to the San Juan Islands from Bellingham, Washington. It was a cloudy day, not too cold, with a nice north wind blowing, giving us a down wind sail for the twenty-five miles home. There were no other boats out. After crossing the five mile wide Rosario Strait, we headed into Peavine Pass, between Blakely and Obstruction Islands. Usually this is one of the spots to motor through; today we could sail.

Tuggy, the ship's cat, was curled up in a ball, sleeping under a down vest in his official spot on the bridge deck by the side of the companion way. Tuggy had been a surprise gift to me from old friends, and was turning into a very seaworthy cat. He rarely went below while we were underway, and was not upset with motoring, sailing in the rain or heavy weather. Tuggy enjoyed going for shore leave, either on his own or on walks with me down the beach or through the woods. Like a well-trained dog, Tuggy came to me when I whistled.

As I looked ahead to see the wind patterns through the pass , I saw spouts and dorsal fins - killer whales were swimming towards us! Keeping track of our approaching courses, I figured we would cross paths near the entrance to the pass. When the orcas were about two hundred feet away, I picked up Tuggy, scratched him under the chin, and set him down on the cabin top facing forward. I said, "Look ahead, Mr.

Cat. Killer whales are going to come by our boat!" In his independent, catlike way, Tuggy looked up at the sails as if to check they were trimmed properly. Then he looked towards Obstruction Island as if to gauge our distance from its rocky shore. Finally he looked astern at Cypress Island, perhaps remembering the day we hiked up Eagle Cliff. Tuggy jumped down into the cockpit, walked to his spot and began to wash himself. "Oh no, Mr. Cat. This is a unique opportunity. You've never seen killer whales before - and they probably have not seen an all gray cat with yellow eyes."

Once more I picked Tuggy up and placed him on the cabin top facing forward. The whales, at least seven of them, were now one hundred feet away. The sound of their blows could be heard as we sailed silently along towards them and the pass. Again the first thing Tuggy did was look up at the sails. Then he gazed over the side at the water flowing past us. And again, he looked astern to watch a glaucous-winged gull soar down to water level and high into the air. I told him, "Tuggy, you do not want to miss this chance to see these whales. But it is your choice of where you look."

Tuggy then jumped down to the deck on the side of the boat that the whales were going to swim past on, and slowly walked aft by the sides of the cockpit. He sat down low on the deck looking out behind the weather cloths. Tuggy's head was extending over the side of the boat when the whale in the lead surfaced directly alongside us, fifty feet away. The cat instantly crouched down as low as he could get to the deck. His eyes were wide open. The whales continued swimming by as we sailed into the pass. The closest orca was thirty feet away when she surfaced and rolled onto her side to look at the boat. She seemed to be focusing on the area where Tuggy was - his eyes certainly were glued on the whale!

I watched it all, standing up on the cockpit seat while steering the sailboat, taking a few photos as the whales swam by. I am glad I took a picture of what Tuggy did next. He had been on deck watching the whales. Above him, lashed to the mizzen mast stays, was my ten speed bicycle. After the whales swam by Tuggy climbed up onto the bike. He stepped onto one of the pedals, then the water bottle cage on the down tube, and up onto the handle bars! He set himself with one back foot where the stem meets the bars and the other foot balancing himself to the right, with his tail out to the left. He sat up on his haunches and held onto the wire stay with his left front paw, and from this elevated position Tuggy watched the whales.

When the whales' fins were small specks in the distance, Tuggy carefully lowered himself to the deck, walked into the cockpit and rubbed against me with a small 'Meow.' Then he went back to his spot and washed himself before curling up into a ball under his down vest and falling asleep. He was purring loudly.

Tuggy watching the whales

Photo: Peter Fromm

Minke Tales

Water Skiing

Lyssa Tall worked for the University of Washington's College of Forest Resources at their research and demonstration forest for three years, where she developed an environmental education and interpretive program for local schools. In 1997, Lyssa started a private consulting business in environmental education.

In the summer of 1989, I was traveling on a ship through the Spice Islands in Indonesia with my grandmother. One day I went water skiing behind a Zodiac with some of the crew from the ship. We were in a strait between several islands, one of which was Komodo Island. It was very warm, the water was flat and calm, perfect water skiing conditions. I skied until my arms got tired, then let go of the rope and got aboard the Zodiac.

As I was toweling off, the guy who was driving the boat looked down. His eyes got really big and his mouth opened wide, but he did not make any sounds. I turned to look and saw a minke whale surface ten feet away from us. The whale was at least twice the size of the Zodiac! We both were surprised and almost fell over.

Then we heard laughter coming from the people on the ship. We thought our surprise at seeing the whale right next to us was what they found funny. When we got back to the ship, my grandmother told us the whale had been porpoising behind me the whole time I was skiing - and neither of us had seen it!

It seemed as if once we had seen the whale, it lost interest in us. Or maybe, since I was no longer water skiing, it did not have anybody to play with and swam away.

Baby Sitting

Maryke DeBoer is a student of biology, specializing in marine life forms. She worked three summers in Greece on a sea turtle project.

In 1996, I went to Scotland to take photo identification and hydrophone recordings of minke whales. Minkes make a fabulous noise which, as far as the researchers knew, had never been recorded. The sounds are a bit like booms which get deeper, slower and longer. There are no squeaks or anything, just booms.

We observed a minke whale with her baby. The mother whale came up to a tour boat and left her baby behind. Perhaps the mom wanted to go for a deep dive for food. She stayed away for half an hour. Meanwhile, the baby was having a splendid time swimming around the boat. Of course, the tourists on the boat were having an even greater time because the young whale was spyhopping and circling around them.

When the mom came back for her little one, the baby did not want to swim away with her! The mother surfaced and swam near her calf, then turned towards the open sea. The baby stayed beside the boat as her mom repeated this several times. Finally, the mom came up between her calf and the boat and pushed the baby along the surface away from the boat. Then they dove and were gone.

Put in Our Place

Dan Harpole has been a resident of Port Townsend, Washington since 1981, and is currently a Jefferson County Commissioner. He is the chair of the Washington State Arts Commission, and former Assistant Director of Centrum, an arts and education organization based in Port Townsend.

After I graduated from Evergreen College and made the decision to stay in the San Juan Islands, I worked at Lonesome Cove Resort on Spieden Channel. Three channels meet off the Resort: Spieden, San Juan and President. Through my work at The Whale Museum I had become interested in minke whales, and knew that where these three channels met was called 'Minke Lake.' It was one of those unbelievably beautiful glassy summer days that only happen a few times a year. I had the day off work and three women friends were visiting. We decided to go out looking for minke whales.

We got into a sixteen foot Boston Whaler, headed east to Jones Island State Park, and hiked up the west facing hill to watch for whales. I thought I saw something to the north, in President Channel off Point Disney on Waldron Island. It was just a dot in the mist, almost two miles away. We were all really enthused about finding a whale, so we went towards it.

For the next two hours, we played cat and mouse with a minke whale. We saw him surface and spout. We roared over, outboard at full throttle, to where the whale had been. Then we would wait, see him spout again some distance away, and chase, roar, and wait again.

Soon we saw two minkes coming together off Point Disney. We realized that the outboard motor was disturbing the grace of the moment. We decided to wait and relax in the boat with the motor off, a quarter of a mile from the whales.

After about thirty minutes our impatience started building. Then we saw a minke spout an eighth of a mile away. I fired up the noisy motor and we were off in pursuit for about a hundred feet when all of a sudden we realized how futile our approach was. How could we be smarter than the whale about where he was going to surface?

We felt silly about it. We again decided to stop and wait. At last, we started to enjoy the beauty of the day in the islands. As we were warmed by the summer sun, we took off our sweaters, and settled into a more receptive mode. We lost our aggressive 'chase' attitude. We felt embarrassed that we had been acting this way around the whales.

I propped myself up against the outboard motor on the back of the boat. We were relaxing, being thankful to have been as close as we had to the whales. We had gone out on a lark, and it was rewarding to have seen two minkes.

We were about to head back to San Juan Island when, with no warning, we heard a phenomenal roar of water breaking open two feet behind the boat. There was a tremendous noise right next to me, as if somebody came into your house in the middle of the night and turned the stereo up full volume. I turned my head to see the water opening up right behind the outboard. A full grown minke whale was spyhopping five feet out of the water.

The whale's incredible eye, only a few feet away, rolled around and distinctly looked at each of us. Time stopped. The minke slid back into the water. It was a terrifying and joyful moment. We were all shouting at each other.

The whale then swam along the starboard side of the sixteen foot boat. He was twenty-five or thirty feet long. He spyhopped and nearly hit the bow. He came up five feet out of the water once more, and we all made eye contact with him again. It was so bright that I saw my reflection in the whale's eye. It was an unforgettable image. Then the whale went back under water.

It was memorable for all of us to see so clearly and closely the minke's big, beautiful black eye rolling around deliberately looking at each of us.

Adrenaline shot through us. The minke swam slowly by the port side. Just as he got to the stern of the boat he came up to the surface, gave a huge blow and sprayed us with fishy smelling mist. Then he dove deep and we never saw him again.

It was a powerful experience. We started up the motor and slowly went back. We felt that our receptivity, rather than our aggressiveness, had allowed this to happen.

I've talked with some of these friends within the last year and we always bring this story up. One friend said it was one of the most joyous and humbling experiences of her life.

We all felt like we had been put in our place.

Escort

Diana Reischel earned a Bachelors Degree in Marine Biology from UC Santa Cruz. She is an accomplished SCUBA diver. Diana has always loved dolphins and whales, and is very active in efforts to protect marine mammals.

I had gone sailing with friends for the weekend to Santa Cruz Island in the Channel Islands of Southern California. We were on our way back to the mainland in the early afternoon. There was just a light wind, so we were motor sailing. The water was flat, visibility was good, but we did not see any wildlife. It was disappointing as we see dolphins on almost every crossing, and often sight whales.

George was steering the boat while we were eating lunch in the cockpit. He yelled, "Oh my God. There's something big and black right next to the boat!"

I was in a bit of a daze, numbed by listening to the droning of the motor and eating good food. I took a moment to react, then I looked. A huge creature spouted alongside of us. It was a whale. I ran inside the cabin, grabbed my camera, and was out on deck again before the whale had taken his next breath. He was swimming parallel to the boat, which was thirty-two feet long. We guessed the whale to be about sixteen feet. When the whale surfaced, he was so close all I could see was his blowhole. I thought I knew this whale, but it took me a little time to think of which one he was.

He turned on his side, and I could see the pectoral fin - it was a minke whale. I only seen photos of minkes. To have one right beside the boat was amazing.

There are many oil rig platforms in the middle of Santa Barbara Channel. We use them as reference marks when making the crossing. The whale swam with the boat the entire distance to platform *Gina,* which took at least two hours. He would surface alongside the bow of the boat, then dive under and come up on the other side. The whale would go back and forth several times under the bow, then dive and swim to the stern of the boat and surface there. The whale repeated this for two hours.

We were moving all over the boat taking pictures of the whale. I was sitting at the tip of the bow, in the pulpit, with my feet over the side, waiting for him. I had been watching his pattern of swimming, so the camera was aimed and focused ahead of the boat where he had been surfacing. I got a picture of him when he came up to breathe.

Once when he surfaced, George yelled that the whale was looking at me. The whale had rolled onto his side and, in fact was watching me. He swam with us for a little longer after that, but soon started to get further away from the boat. He disappeared just before we got to platform *Gina*. This area between the islands and the oil platforms are the vessel traffic lanes, where the large cargo boats travel. We called the whale our 'escort' to get across the lanes.

Surfacing minke whale

Humpback Tales

The Day of the Whales

Megan Bailiff did research for her Masters Degree in Biological Oceanography in the Antarctic. She was part of an interdisciplinary research program called RACER (Research on Antarctic Coastal Ecosystem Rates), designed to understand the mechanisms which give rise to the extraordinarily high productivity of the coastal shelf ecosystem of the Antarctic Peninsula.

Megan is now with the Washington Sea Grant Program based at the University of Washington. She works with both State and Federal legislators to keep the program funded by expounding on its merits and importance to both the marine-scientific and marine-user communities.

I had an encounter with the whales while at Palmer Station in the Antarctic, located on Anvers Island near the Bransfield Strait. This is the smaller of the two U.S. Stations there. My experience took place on what is now known as *The Day of the Whales*: March 4, 1987 (which also happened to be my 26th birthday). I was in the Antarctic conducting my Masters thesis research.

On one of the few occasions that our science crew was at the Palmer Station (rather than collecting samples on the ship) We had the opportunity to go out exploring in one of the Zodiac rafts. We took off in the morning to look at some of the nearby islands. Every Zodiac is required to carry a walkie-talkie to maintain contact with the base and other boats for safety. A short time into our adventuring we heard a distress call from another boat. The message was a garbled: "Help...help...Oh...My...God..." We were about five minutes away and sped to where they were. As we came around an iceberg, we saw a humpback whale spyhopping halfway out of the water next to the Zodiac. The people in the raft were okay. They were concerned that the whale was going to tip over their boat. If you get tipped over into Antarctic water you are as good as dead. By the time we got there, they had realized the whale was just playing with them, and was sensitive to where their boat was.

The humpback was going underneath the Zodiac and rubbing his back, then lifting his head out of the water next to the boat. He seemed to be asking to be touched and the guys in the boat were glad to accommodate.

Humpback near Palmer Station   Photo: Dave Jones

There was another humpback nearby and when the whales heard the motor of our Zodiac approaching, they swam over to see us. It turned out the whales had been feeding in this area and were now playing with us, too. During the five hours this encounter lasted, we kept bringing other people out from Palmer Station. With each new boatload, the whales would swim over and check out the new arrivals.

At one point, one of the whales swam beneath the boat I was in, turned upside down and brought both his pectoral fins out of the water on either side of the boat. Fifteen feet long, weighing two thousand pounds each, they towered over us, waving slightly. The whale then gently raised our boat with six people in it out of the water, on his belly. Then he slowly submerged and we were floating again.

A few times the whales raised their tail flukes and dumped a little water into the Zodiacs. Apparently they were not trying to harm us, rather just playing. It was as if the whales were aware that if they were too rough they would tip us over. Finally the whales were ready to leave. We followed them for a few miles as they swam back out to sea.

When we got back to the ship, there was a line to use the darkroom and develop the film which had been shot. Everyone was talking about how close they were: reaching out and touching the whales, looking in their eyes and having them look back.

Humpback spyhopping in Antarctica   Photo: Dave Jones

When I got back to Hawaii, where humpback whales spend a lot of time, I talked with people I knew who work with them. Up until then in their professional careers they had never heard of whales soliciting the kind of interaction I had encountered in the Antarctic. Whales are not necessarily shy if you go up to them, but humpbacks rarely come and seek out the kind of encounter we had experienced. All the interactions we had were initiated by the whales.

The scientists thought there must have been a krill mass which came ashore and attracted the whales to feed. They must have gotten curious about the humans in the Zodiacs.

There are now several enlarged photographs on the wall at Palmer Station and a sign which reads: *The Day of the Whales.* Everyone who goes to Palmer Station hears the story of that famous day.

Center Yourself

Urmas Kaldveer is an instructor at Mendocino Community College in Ukiah, California. He has been teaching environmental science and concepts of biology for twenty years. He has also been a carpenter and professional diver for the Bodega Marine Laboratory.

My first whale experience was in 1971 when I was working with the Bodega Marine Laboratory. I was doing plankton trawls collecting sea life for them in Bodega Bay on a thirty-six foot powerboat.

I noticed that a fog bank seemed to be approaching, but I thought it would not come in for some time - which was a big mistake. Before I could even think about it, I was enveloped in a very dense fog.

I was scared. I did not have radar, and I was not an experienced seaman. The fog was extremely thick. I could hear the surf crashing against the rocks. I began to lose orientation, and felt on the edge of panic. I heard a large sound. A humpback whale breached about fifty feet in front of the boat. I saw the dark-skinned whale clearly against the fog.

It was surrealistic. My whole world was light gray, with nothing differentiating the sky from the sea. I saw a whale leap into the gray air, then plunge into the gray water.

I calmed down enough so I could focus on what had to be done. I put out a sea anchor and kept checking the fathometer. I looked at the compass and studied the chart. I was able to pay attention to those details which are important to a mariner in the fog.

I feel that part of the reason I was able to stay focused on the task at hand was because the presence of the whale reassured me that I was not alone. I only saw it the one time. An hour or so later the fog cleared and I went in.

That was my first whale experience, and it was twenty-two years until the next one. I was diving near Ziuatenaho, Mexico, by a small cove. I came to the surface, looked out at the ocean, and suddenly had an enormously strong draw. It was almost like a voice saying, "Get back to the ocean." What I saw at that moment was whales. Somehow, I thought, the whales were saying this.

My wife, Susan, came out of the water. I said, "You won't believe what I am going through; I am having a powerful feeling."

Over dinner we both agreed that while it was very interesting, my days of being out at the ocean and dealing with whales was over. I had a job, a home, and a family. I was not about to go out to sea, or so I thought.

Within two weeks of the time we got back to Ukiah, the cosmos began working its amazing ways: the next thing I knew I was Executive Director of *Pelagikos*, a nonprofit research organization with a seventy-two foot sailboat designed for oceanic travel and studies.

And we are about to leave for nine months of research.

Breaching Lessons

Sue Muloin is a lecturer at a university in Australia. For the last couple of years she has been working on her Ph.D. in wildlife tourism with a specific emphasis on whale watching. Consequently, Sue has seen many whales in the last two years in Australia, the United States and Canada.

In Queensland, Australia there is an area called Hervey Bay, considered to be the best place in the world to see humpback whales. These are southern humpbacks, so they have white bellies. Northern humpbacks have black bellies. Other than that, they are the same species, but they have not interbred. They are two subspecies of the same mammal.

A lot of times whales come in the bay and the mothers are not feeding. They are resting and trying to fatten up their calves with their rich milk. We get about three to four hundred humpbacks in the area. The rest of the whales are on their way south, back to the Antarctic to feed. On their northbound route they swim to the Great Barrier Reef where they mate and give birth. The mothers and calves come through last because they need to get enough blubber on their bodies before they reach the colder Antarctic waters. So they come through slower to allow that build up, especially on the calves. An adult humpback has a meter (40 inches) of blubber around it.

I was out on a whale watch boat collecting data, which involved giving questionnaires to people aboard and taking notes on what the whales were doing. I remember this incident very clearly because I

Hervey Bay, Queensland, Australia   *Photo: Mark Farrel*

was busy recording the whales' behavior. We approached a mother and her calf who were breaching. The calf was probably four-to-eight weeks old. It was very early in the morning, and there were no other boats around. When we got close to them, the whales kept breaching. They would not stop. I counted over 160 breaches by the mother and calf. Each time she breached, the calf got a bit better at it. The first few times she was doing belly flops, head stands, half a body out, backwards. But after a while we could see her breaching style improve. The mother was teaching that behavior to her calf.

We stayed with them for an hour. We went to watch another group of whales and then left the bay. The mother and her calf were still breaching when we left. I kept an accurate count of the number of breaches. It continued nonstop.

The people in the boat were very excited to be witnessing such a wonderful sight. One man dropped his camera into the water, but did not seem too upset about losing it. ⌣

Too Friendly

Eric Martin is a well known whale and dolphin photographer, based in Southern California.

Whale Tales' cover photo is by Eric, showing Chris Carson videoing the tail of the whale that splashed him and his friend.

For the past twenty years, every weekend I go out into the ocean, travel the same route, making a 'transit,' and document what marine mammals I see. From the charts, I learned where underwater canyons and mountain ranges were located, and how upwellings and currents in the ocean affected food distribution and determined whales' routes.

I have been observing humpback whales for many years, photographing their tail flukes as part of a census. I work to be as unobtrusive as possible. I know the animals do not like your boat close alongside or behind them. Humpbacks want to see what is going on. If you get behind a humpback and they cannot see you, they don't know what is back there and they get a little hesitant. When I see an animal I go slowly, staying a distance away, not even taking photos.

Quite a few times animals do not want you around. They can be moody. If they want to be left alone, I leave them alone and go find another one - there are plenty of them out there!

In 1985 we had a friendly encounter with a whale. He lifted his head and looked over the boat, as if to say hello. Humpbacks have very different personalities. This one was very calm; all he did after watching us from a spyhop was float beneath our boat and look up.

A week later we ran across two humpbacks who simply circled out boat. We just sat there. The whales were curious about us but not enough to come close. After photographing them, we left to see what else we could find.

All of a sudden we met up with two other humpback whales. They started circling our stopped boat like they were curious. They went down for about five minutes, and we did not see anything.

I looked over the side of the boat, right into the face of a very large female. She was interested in us. She would look at us, then swish her tail under the boat making a big commotion, her tail coming within inches of us!

Then she lifted up fifty to sixty gallons of water with her tail and lobbed it over the side of the boat, right onto us! She stuck her head out of the water to see exactly the effect of her shot. Then she did it again. The whale's behavior was intentional.

We were not sure if it was aggression, because she was making 'trumpet' blows, which can mean aggression or communication with another whale. The whale might have been trying to communicate with us. She would lay on the surface of the water, close behind the boat on her back, flopping her pectoral fins back and forth on the water. That is not the sign of an aggressive whale.

After four or five dumps from her tail, she turned on her side and swam next to us. Her tail flukes went by up in the air inches from the side of the boat. She was so close I could touch her. I do not like to touch wild animals, but it seemed as if this whale was longing for attention, so I reached out as she swam by. I lost my balance when the boat lurched from her wake. As I was about to fall overboard, the side of the whale's tail hit my hand and pushed me back up into the boat.

Did she know I was going into the water and try to keep me on the boat? Or was it just a fortunate accident? She kept me from falling - that's all I know.

A friend was also out there in his boat. We talked on the radio and I asked if he was interested in seeing a friendly whale.

He is a very good friend; we play practical jokes on each other all the time. He is a very neat, well-groomed guy.

He was a few miles away and we began to motor slowly in my friend's direction. The whale followed us. Someone on my boat suggested that we stop and see what the whale did next. So we stopped, in neutral with the engine still on.

The whale came up alongside us, looked at us, went down and gave us the ultimate splash of splashes. A hundred gallons, right in the boat! All over us. Water was all over the boat. Both bilge pumps were going. Two of the three VHF radios were dead.

I felt this was enough. We got going again and the whale kept following us until my friend showed up half an hour later.

I pointed the whale out to him, then gunned the engine because the whale was coming to my boat, following us rather than my friend's. I sped up and got about a hundred yards away from the whale.

The humpback became involved with my friend's boat. My friend had his cameras out. I called him on our last working radio and said,

"Put your camera gear away! Trust me!" I did not tell him why, and he had no idea what to expect.

He thought it was great. The whale was sticking her head up, looking at him, turning on her side, splashing her pectoral fins close to his boat, and sizing him up.

All of a sudden, 'Wooosshhh!' goes her tail. He got a salt water shower like us. His yachting clothes got soaked, his neat hair was washed with a wave! The whale splashed him a couple of times. Three hours later, as if somebody was calling, the whale took off and swam away. That is how it ended.

I want to share my knowledge about the ocean and marine mammals, on a deeper level than when I give talks and show photographs. I have begun wildlife nature tours, taking people out on full day boat trips to see what is really out there. Hopefully the encounters people have will give them great memories and appreciation of those creatures who share this part of the planet with us.

There is something special about being with the whales and dolphins. There is an aura, there is magic. If your heart is in the right place for being out on the water with these animals, they will show you a lot. You just have to open your heart and ears.

Gray Whale Tales

You Again?

Bruce Williams and Susan Speck own Dolphin Dive Center in Arcadia, California. They are photojournalists who have worked in the diving industry for many years. Susan recently published a diving guide for the Baja Peninsula in Mexico.

Berington Van Campen has been diving for over thirty years. He composes music for film and television. This led to a project with the Handicapped SCUBA Association with Jean Michel Cousteau. Since then Berington's underwater camera works and music credits include a number of Discovery Channel Specials, including: Seals, Whales and Dolphin Tales. *His work was also on an episode of ABC's* Treasure! *series, about Mel Fisher and the search for the shipwrecked* Atocha.

Bruce: Sometime ago, before we went to Baja to see the gray whales, I was making a dive at Laguna Beach. I came to a reef rising from the ocean floor. On it was an unusual keyhole limpet. I poked it, and it closed up while I watched. I had never seen a limpet close the orifice on its peak. Just as it did, the whole reef moved. I thought we were having an earthquake. All of a sudden, I realized the whole reef was moving towards me, and I saw there were barnacles on it.

All the kelp along the bottom started to lay down and drag along with the reef. I looked to the right to the end of the reef and saw a whale's tail going up and down. Underneath the tail was streaming milk, and a baby whale's tail was on the other side, also going up and down.

I guessed I had poked a nursing gray whale right in the eye with my finger while she was laying on the bottom in about thirty feet of water. I swam down fast to the sea bed. I thought her tail was going to smack my head, but it went right over me, and they swam away.

Berington: We made three trips to Baja California to see the gray whales. On the first trip, we went to Scammon's Lagoon and learned that you had to have the right tools for the job, and that you cannot sneak in past the Federales!

The right tool was not the inflatable boat we brought; it did not have the proper-sized floor boards, so the boat would bend in half at the middle. We jury-rigged it and tried to get out into the Lagoon just after the sun came up. Because of the tides, the water was right by our campsite at

Bruce Williams with gray whale   Photo: Susan Speck

night, but in the morning it was about a quarter of a mile away.

We slogged across the mud towing the rubber boat on its wheels. Eventually we got out to the water's edge. Two guys came running out into the water and stopped us in our tracks. Federales. The Mexican Government wants to control access to the breeding grounds of these whales so that they are not harassed, which is good.

In 1992, on our second trip, we were successful in getting out in San Ignacio Lagoon in our own boat. We got into the water and went snorkeling with a gray whale mother and her calf. I saw a huge back go under the water heading towards me. Bruce was telling me to turn on my video camera because there was a whale right under me. I looked down and around, but did not see any whale. The visibility was not that great. Bruce kept telling me to turn on the camera and shoot. At last I did, and just shot into the water below me. I panned around as if I was filming a whale.

When I looked at the video tape at home, there was the whale! She was directly below me and so close and big I could not see the edges of her, and we need edges to define what we are looking at.

Bruce: There was a little bit of wind so the water was choppy. I was standing in the boat as it was rocking. The boat seemed to be moving more than it should have for the size of the waves. All of a sudden, Susan and Berington's eyes got really big as they were looking at me. Berington yelled at me to turn around. I did, and was eye-to-eye with a spyhopping gray whale! There were about eight feet of head sticking up out of the water next to me. Her eye was two feet away from mine. For a split second I was frozen with fear from the memory of poking that nursing whale's eye years earlier at Laguna Beach.

My fear went away in a heart beat as I looked at her eye. It was the size of an orange and had a beautiful brown color. It had nice eyelashes and whale lice running around by it. Her barnacles were catching on the rub rail of the inflatable, jerking it around. That was what had caused the boat to rock so much.

It was very quiet around there. Even though there was no malice in the whale's eye, I realized I was not in control. We were about seven miles out into the lagoon, totally at the mercy of the mother and her baby. She was very gentle. She slowly slid back down into the water and they swam off.

Berington: We got back the next year, and hired one of the local fishermen to take us out. His name was Chima, and he seemed to have some sort of rapport with these whales. They knew him and the sound of his engine. And he was loving and respectful towards them. Chima would say, "Come on baby, push the boat!" He was always talking to the whales.

The whales also liked the sound of the outboard, so he never shut it off. He said that is how they knew he was there.

I do not know what caused it, but we had at least four to five hours of nonstop interactions with whales that day with Chima. The mother whale would lift the two thousand pound, wooden, twenty-four foot panga clear up out of the water on her back and carry us for a hundred yards!

The whales gravitated towards Chima's boat from another boat. As soon as Chima got out with us aboard, the whales came over. After a short time, the other boat left.

Bruce: Berington got a little whale snot in his camera and on his face from her blowing so close to us.

The baby came in and interacted with us. While the mother did not seem to encourage her baby, she did not stop him from coming and checking us out. We were able to pet him. We pulled some lice out from around the baby's eyes. He seemed to like that. He would roll over on his back and we could see the pleats in his throat. The mother did the same thing. We were able to reach down into the furrows and dig lice and barnacles out. Her blowhole was encrusted enough on one side that her exhaust was restricted. I was able to reach over and grab hold of a whole hunk of barnacles and rip them out. The blowhole is pretty strong. When that thing closes up, you better not have your fingers in there. She slapped it shut a couple of times when she was close to us. You could tell from her body movements that she appreciated our getting those things out of there. I was really amazed at how deep barnacles actually imbed themselves in the whale's skin.

Berington: On one side of the boat twenty feet behind us you could see the head. About thirty feet in front of us on the other side you see the tail flukes! And it seemed the lagoon was full of whales.

The mom would roll over so slowly she would rotate onto her back and hold her pectoral fins flat out as if she surrendered. She would come up often to Chima, who kissed her on the nose, again and again.

Bruce: Whales are aware of how much space they take up, and what their radius is. We know we can reach out just so far; it is the same thing for them. When they are in close, around a boat, they will fold down a pectoral fin or roll so they do not hit the boat. It is the same with the tail flukes. It looks like it is going to smack you, then the flukes go right on by, never touching a thing. They know exactly where they end, forty feet behind them.

Berington: And yet, they seemed like very tactile creatures to us. They touched the boat at every opportunity, and let us touch them. At one point, the mother rolled up next to the side of the boat and opened her mouth so we could rub her lips and baleen.

When they roll over and look up at you with that eye they are *looking* at you. It is not just the direction the eye is going - they are

Gray whale and friends   *Photo: Susan Speck*

looking straight through you. There is no doubt that there is a very intelligent brain in there that is curious about who we are and what we are doing floating around in their home. When we were with the whales they were playful, calm and relaxed. It seemed they enjoyed their time with us as much as we did with them. 🐋

Scarback

Carrol Zumwalt has worked in the charter fishing industry since moving to the Oregon Coast from Portland in 1982. She is currently employed at Tradewind Charters in Newport.

We nicknamed one of the gray whales off Newport, Oregon *Scarback*. The first time we knew she was around was in 1992. One of our skippers, Del Wilkison, was on a five hour fishing trip on the thirty-eight foot boat *Northwinds*. When he came, in his eyes were as big as saucers, and he was almost white with fear. "Good God! I just had a whale run me right off the ocean! That whale got so close you could not have put tissue paper between the boat and him!"

The next day we sent a boat out whale watching. I had a lady come into the office intent on seeing whales. She wanted me to guarantee it, but I told her we couldn't. Her husband really wanted to go, and she finally consented to go with no guarantee. They went out on the *Ilwaco Indian*.

When they got out there, *Scarback* came right up to the boat and spyhopped. The woman got to pet the whale. When she came back in, she was six feet off the ground, jumping around and screaming about how she petted a whale. I do not know what kind of connections she had, but shortly after that we had all the Portland TV stations there, and apparently CNN picked up one of those broadcasts because they came out, too. Their footage showing the whale coming right up next to the *Ilwaco Indian* went all over the United States.

The Captain would take the boat out, turn the engines off and just drift in the ocean. The whale would come up, rub on the boat and swim under it.

We had another gal go out there and the whale came far enough out of the water that she put her hands around him and gave the whale a big kiss. She said it wasn't slimy, just rubbery. She didn't know whales had whiskers, and neither did I at the time, but there they were.

Scarback had a great big scar in the middle of her back. Three years before, whales had been trapped in the ice near Barrow, Alaska. We felt she might have been the one that was injured. Rescuers had kept the whale calm by petting her, so as to keep her from further hurting herself. For whatever reason, this whale absolutely loved people.

For years we have been taking folks out to see the gray whales on their migration. There were usually never whales in the area during the summer. *Scarback* started showing up in the summer, and would stay around until September. Then she left. We wondered where she went. We saw in *The Oregonian* newspaper that she had swum up to Seattle.

The next year she came back and it was the same thing all over again, only she had four or five other whales with her. They stayed in the area and fed all summer long.

Two autumns ago, I went out on the last whale watching trip of the season. I saw a little more whale than I wanted. They were mating. All we could see was rolling and splashing, and the male. This year *Scarback* returned with a calf by her side. This made us realize she was a female.

Because of all the publicity the interactions generated, we received a letter from the Federal government. They warned us about 'harassing the whales' and wrote down all the guidelines and fines we could be liable for. We were not chasing the whales. You go out there and stop the boat and the whales come to you. It would not make any difference where *Scarback* was in the ocean. When the boat got there, she was there too. This was especially the case for the *Ilwaco Indian*. She would come around other boats, but there was something about the bottom of that boat that she would like to rub up against. She would turn the boat in a circle by rubbing against it. It was exciting to be so close to such a huge, gentle animal. I get chills just thinking about it.

There was nothing we could do about the issue with the marine mammal officials. We were not supposed to touch her. We let all our guests know ahead of time they could not touch the whale. If she wanted to rub on the boat, she would.

Shortly after we got the letter from the Government, reporters interviewed me on TV. They asked if I considered our actions to be harassment. I told them when that big of a mammal comes up to you and starts rubbing on your boat, you can't say, "Shoo, get away from here, whale!" They will do what they want to do. ◁

Their Favorite Boat

Doris Ross is a retired hospital administrator and a licensed vocational nurse. Her husband worked for the California State Department of Education. They have enjoyed numerous trips with many organizations including Elderhostel, and are particularly fond of outdoor activities. Doris and her husband have canoed down the Colorado River and in the Boundary Waters of Minnesota. They especially love watching birds and other wildlife wherever they travel.

In 1987, my husband and I went on a whale watching trip with the American Cetacean Society out of San Diego. We traveled to San Ignacio Lagoon in Baja, Mexico. We sighted a number of whales on the way down there, always at a distance. As we got closer to the lagoon, we saw whales spyhopping.

We had been told by the naturalists on the ship that within the past few years gray whales had begun to exhibit 'friendly' behavior, that is, whales coming up to people in boats. We talked about it and hoped that we might see it.

The naturalists also said that skiffs used to go out into the lagoon

Gray whale and hand   Photo: Jacque Ross

would have small motors on them. At that time the only reported accident had been between a whale and a boat with oars. It was as though
the motor would let the whale know we were there. Eight people went
out in these skiffs, with a Mexican fisherman operating the little motor.
Two skiffs with people from our boat were in the lagoon.

The first time we went out, we saw a lot of spyhopping and whales
come close to us. In fact, a cow and a calf came right beside our skiff.
I put my hand into the mother's mouth and felt her baleen. The second
time out, we suddenly had eight or ten whales around us.

The other skiff was at least two hundred yards away. There were
no whales around it. The whales dove under us. One of them lifted the
boat gently out of the water, then slowly lowered us down. Our skiff
operator said he had never seen so many whales around his boat. He
said it was too frightening; there were too many whales, and he did not
know what to expect. He gently eased over to the other skiff to see if
some of the whales would stay with that boat. The whales continued to
circle, spyhop and go under our skiff. They would turn sideways and
look at us. When we got fairly close, several of the whales began to
nudge us back, pushing our skiff away from the other boat. We could

not do anything about it. The whales obviously did not want to be over there, and they did not want us to be over there, either. And that's the way it turned out.

It was a strange experience to have the whales treat our boat like a little bathtub toy! This went on for thirty minutes, perhaps longer, before they slipped below the surface, spyhopped one last time, and left us alone. The whales never went to the other skiff. As far as we could tell, the two skiffs were identical. They had the same kind of motor, and there were eight people in each. No one ever figured out why they liked our skiff so much more. ⋖

We Saw a Whale!

Lyssa Tall runs a private consulting business in environmental education. She also has a story about a minke whale on page 17.

I have seen lots of whales, but my first experience with a whale in the wild was the most moving. It was in the summer time. I was fifteen years old and visiting some friends who have a beach house on Hood Canal, along the east side of the Olympic Peninsula in Washington. One warm evening we were watching the sunset from a rocky outcropping. The tide was high, the water was just a few feet below us and perfectly clear.

My friend Nina, her mother Helen and I were sitting quietly, in our own private worlds, watching the sunset over the Olympic Mountains. All of a sudden, Nina yelled. I turned towards her. She was looking down at the water. There was a young gray whale gliding past, no more than ten feet from us.

The first thing that registered were the flukes. What went through my mind was: "Really big fish!" Then I realized it was a whale. I was so surprised that I almost fell into the water. We watched the whale glide by silently. It came up and blew, then sounded and was gone.

We were stunned and continued to sit there for half an hour in silence as the sun set. That night Nina and I kept each other up by repeating, "Can you believe we saw a whale?" We were in awe for the next three days. We walked around in a daze going, "We saw a whale! Oh wow! We saw a whale!" It touched a place deep inside of us, and made us feel like we were connected to something a lot bigger than just ourselves. ⋖

¡Otra Mas!

Terry Domico *makes his living as a naturalist and nature photographer. He is a specialist in field biology and natural history. He is currently working on the natural history of a jungle tree in Malaysia, which may have medicinal use in western culture. Terry has written several coffee table photography books, including:* Bears Of The World; Kangaroos, The Marvelous Mob; *and,* Borneo.

Two friends and I went to Baja California in Mexico to photograph gray whales. I had heard about 'friendly behavior,' in which gray whales reportedly approached boats and interacted with the people in them.

This has become quite famous both in the San Ignacio Lagoon and Bahia Magdalena, where boat traffic is highly controlled by the Mexican government. A permit is required to get in, and there is little choice of what to do or where to go. We traveled to both areas and went out in open twenty-four foot fishing boats called pangas, driven by Mexican fishermen. Unfortunately, we did not observe any specific friendly behavior.

On our way to Cabo San Lucas, we camped on the beach at Todos Santos where there were dozens of gray whales feeding within fifty-feet of the shore. While we were watching, a calf swam in between her mother and the shore and got stranded on a sandbar which had deep water around it. She was right there in front of us. The young whale started vocalizing while slamming her tail onto the sand. Three other whales came up and started spyhopping. Then they moved closer and spyhopped again where the mother was. You could see she was concerned. Still in the deep water the mother whale was nuzzling her stranded baby. I heard the adult whales making grunting sounds, and the baby stopped thrashing about.

When the barrel of a wave came in, the young whale lifted up and moved a bit, then settled back down onto the sand. Then the next wave came in and she moved a bit more and settled down again. Meanwhile, all the adult whales were still there with their heads in the breaking surf. After about five waves lifted the young whale, she swam free.

A few days later we went to San Ignacio Lagoon again. It is a difficult lagoon to reach. A fifty-seven kilometer dirt road goes there. It is world class washboard and there is nothing out there on the coast, no facilities of any kind. When it rains the road is not passable. The area is featureless, the shore is sandy and low and disappears in the distance. The lagoon is about eighteen miles long and seven miles across; it is a barren looking area.

It was windy and rainy. One night the wind blew my tent over, with me in it. All the tent pegs came out and I skidded along until the tent collapsed around me. I didn't get much sleep that night.

When we got to the lagoon we met a Mexican fisherman named Antonio. He didn't speak any English. He agreed to take us out around eight in the morning. Most of the other fishermen took people out to look for whales around ten or eleven, after they had gone fishing. They would zoom here and zoom there, then slowly putt-putt around an area, then zoom to a new spot. Antonio was different. He would stop the boat, turn off the motor and sit. Then he would slowly motor us to another spot and turn off the motor again and sit, listening and watching.

There were a lot of whales in the area, and maybe four or five tourist boats with a dozen people in each. We saw some whale interaction happening with people in another boat. We approached the boat slowly from downwind, just watching. A whale broke off from the boat it was with and came over to our boat, right to where I was. I expected the whale to be on the left side of the boat, but he went underneath us and rose out of the water on my right while I was still looking to the left. I turned around to see the head of an adult gray whale towering eight feet above me! The whale leaned his head onto the gunnel so lightly that it barely tipped the boat.

I reached up and touched the whale's lip with my hands. I could feel a bit of a quiver go through the animal's body. It was like petting a wet inner tube. At one point while I was stroking the whale, he opened his mouth and allowed me to touch the baleen plates. They felt like nylon bristles. The whale slid back into the water beside our boat and as I scratched and petted him, he rolled over like a puppy dog. His big pectoral fins went 'Whap' into the water each time he rolled.

Then the whale swam under the boat to Mark, and he started petting it. Next the whale went over to Antonio. Then the whale went to another boat that had drifted towards us. The whale let everyone in the boat pet him. He went from one person to another. They were all lined up at the side of the boat and touched him in their turn. Then the whale slowly swam to a third boat which had joined us and shut down their motor, too. Again, everyone aboard was lined up along the side and the whale surfaced so they could each touch him.

Petting a gray whale in San Ignacio Lagoon   Photo: Terry Domico

The whale broke off from them and was swimming back towards our boat, when a little girl at the end of the line cried, "Mom, I didn't get to pet him!" Then she began to cry out loud. The whale stopped, turned around and swam back to the boat. He brought his head out of the water right next to the little girl. She was surprised, and timidly reached out her small hand to gently touch the giant animal. Perhaps the whale heard her cry and responded as if to a distress call. It intentionally singled her out.

Then the whale dropped back into the water and swam over to our boat again. Both Mark and I were standing. All of a sudden our boat started rocking, and we sat down fast. The people in the two other boats were yelling at us. The whale lifted our boat completely out of the water on his back, then lowered us gently.

The whale came to me one last time, then disappeared. Antonio yelled in Spanish to get ready. All of a sudden, in front of our boat, the full whale, a complete breach! Then a wave came right over top of us. Antonio yelled, "¡Otra Mas!" Again, a full breech! Four more times Antonio yelled, "¡Otra Mas!" and four times right in front of us the whale breached. Then he was gone. Somehow Antonio knew when the whale was about to breach.

I was pretty high from the experience. As a biologist, it intrigued me that there was no reward for this animal to behave like he did, other than the physical contact with humans. The whale was not being fed.

He was not receiving any benefit or punishment for his behavior. He had complete control at all times. He initiated the contact. He broke off the contact when he wanted, and he was totally in charge of the contact all the way through it. The whale chose who he was going to surface next to and when he was going to surface. The whale was very discretionary.

I had never seen anything like it, and I have spent a great deal of time around animals. It was a remarkable series of events to experience with a wild animal.

Dolphin Tales

Don't Worry, Be Happy

Jennifer Durnin has been a marine videographer in Hawaii since 1990. She serves as a naturalist on a diving boat for a nonprofit organization, helping educate divers about coral reefs, reef dwellers and marine mammals.

I was sailing with my boyfriend on a sixty-four foot catamaran off Maui, Hawaii, when the boat broke down. We had no steering. He got really concerned because it seemed out of the question for us to make any repairs. I was starting to get worried that we would not get back in.

From out of nowhere, seven bottlenose dolphins came flying out of the water all around us. As many years as we had lived in Hawaii, we had never seen the kind of jump these dolphins were doing next to our broken-down boat. They were coming out of the water vertically and synchronized, like in a marine park show - not horizontally the way they usually jump. It was like a beautiful dance. I had the strong feeling that the dolphins were there to let us know everything was going to be all right.

We relaxed about our situation, forgetting about being on a boat with no steering, and with wonder and amazement simply watched the dolphins' dance. They were around the boat for ten minutes. After they left, my boyfriend quickly saw an easy way to get the boat's steering operable, and we made it back to her mooring safely.

The two of us felt this was a magical experience. The dolphins came to us just at the time we were feeling the most desperate and doubtful about getting back before dark. It was a very nice feeling that the dolphins' timing was so perfect. The dolphins' dance changed our attitudes and lifted our spirits.

Green!

Bruce Gregg has been a boat builder and Captain. Now he repairs guitars and does design work. He lives on Lopez Island, Washington.

In 1978, we were motoring through the night north from San Diego to Catalina Island. There had been a storm for the past few days, but it calmed down and there was no wind. Even when the Pacific is calm, it is never flat. The water was glassy but rolling slowly with the ever-present ocean swell. It was a very pleasant ride. I was on watch and noticed that behind us, our prop wash was a glowing, brilliant emerald green column of phosphorescence. Little flashes were going off in it, like miniature depth charges.

While the whole crew was on deck watching our green glowing trail, three pairs of dolphins came right at us. At first we did not see the animals themselves, just their phosphorescent trails. They took turns swimming on each side of the boat, then leaped into the air under the bowsprit, crossing in midair as they jumped. Two dolphins would swim off, circle around, and then the next pair would come and repeat that crossing jump. Then the next pair did the same thing.

We took turns laying on the bowsprit watching the dolphins below us. As they jumped out of the water, the dolphins were glowing the same brilliant emerald green, because the phosphorescence was clinging all over their bodies. I could see their eyes turning to look at me as they flew by.

The dolphins swam with us for at least half-an-hour, enough time for everybody on board to get a turn on the bowsprit. We all noticed definite, intentional eye contact. They were looking at us, and we were looking at them. There was being-to-being rapport. It made me feel alive. It was humbling to realize humans are not the only thinking animals on Earth.

If space aliens ever showed up here, looking for the most intelligent species on a planet that was three-quarters water, they would choose whales and dolphins because those animals don't need all the polluting causing accouterments that humans think they need. ⌖

Touch

Walt Taylor grew up near the Pacific Ocean, and started sailing at age 9. He turned 75 in 1999. He has sailed his own boats for most of his life. During World War II, he was an engineering officer in the Merchant Marine. After the war he became an instructor at the Maritime Academy in San Mateo. Walt has explored the Pacific, Atlantic and Indian Oceans.

I was racing in the initial Pacific Cup (the San Francisco to Kauai Race) in June 1980. We sailed into the Pacific High. We did not go far enough south, so we were drifting in the mid-Pacific with very little wind. We were on a Cal-36, with six of us aboard.

I had the early morning watch, and was half asleep. It was about three o'clock on a warm, starry night. The boat had no motion at all. I was not moving a muscle, leaning back in the cockpit, totally relaxed. My left hand was on the tiller and my right hand was hanging over the side of the boat.

I heard a 'Whoosh!' kind of a noise by the side of the boat, turned my head and there, right below my hand, was a dolphin just looking at me - about two feet of him out of the water. I kept my hand where it was and did not move. The dolphin raised up and nuzzled my hand with his face, as would a dog, or horse, or lover.

Then, in a sheer joyous moment, he made a couple of phosphorescent 'torpedo' runs directly at the side of the boat, and a couple of leaps into the air. I heard the splash when his body hit the water and I saw the phosphorescence, but not the dolphin.

I have sailed for some sixty years, and have spent time as a professional mariner. I had never had the experience of feeling that an animal in the wild was trying so hard to communicate with me. Soon after, when I called the next watch, I was almost speechless. I could not describe what happened, it was such a moving and touching experience. Not just because the dolphin physically touched my hand, but because I could feel the presence of a being.

Another dolphin event I witnessed happened when five boats were headed for Santa Cruz Island. A sailor and his girlfriend were on one of the boats. They were about fifty feet from us.

We got into a pod of dolphins. They were swimming all around the boats. Lisa, the girlfriend, got out on the bow pulpit, squealing with delight as the dolphins swam seven feet below her. The dolphins jumped over her first from one side, then the other. She let out more squeals when, about fifty feet ahead of their boat, a dolphin came out of the water standing on his tail. He traveled for about twenty-five yards on his tail, facing back to the boat.

At the time, Lisa was not hooked on sailing: now she is. She tells people the experience with those dolphins was one of the emotional highlights of her life.

Another dolphin behavior several of us have witnessed is the training of young animals by their mom or uncle to 'porpoise' through the water. Mom will lead and if the baby does not follow, one of the adults will nudge it to get it going.

When I saw all this, I realized how intelligent and social these animals are. As experiences like this accumulate, they increased my respect for marine mammals. Being close to Nature, uninterrupted by outside 'civilized' things, emotions and sensitivity seem heightened, as do vision and hearing.

These experiences are all very humbling.

Whales Come to Boats

Thanks!

Lisa Lamb got her Captain's papers in 1987. She owns a Russian built hydrofoil speed boat and takes people out looking for wildlife and whales. Lisa and her husband Neil live on an out island in the San Juans, quieter than the main islands which are ferry served.

We finally got our ninety-eight foot old wooden boat running well enough to go up to Alaska. We had a little machine shop on board so we could work on fish boats. We traveled around to many of the little backwater ports.

We came south in the Fall, after the Equinox. You have to go 'Outside' at two places on the 'Inside' passage. One of the places is by Egg Island. We came around there, and the Pacific Ocean just beat us up. We were rolling sideways in the troughs the whole way. We were really tired - it was a long run that day, about twelve hours through rough water. We got down to some bays where one could anchor and be safe. We picked one off Nigei Island, a place called Alexander Bay, a big bay right across from 'God's Pocket.'

We turned the corner to go in, and my husband Neil said, "Look! There's life!" We could not figure out what name to put on them, because they looked like porpoise tails standing up. Two identical black tails about a foot above the water and about a foot apart. They were just standing straight up and wiggling. We had never seen a harbor porpoise do that. We thought they could be Dall's porpoises, but I'd never seen a Dall's porpoise do that either.

We cruised over that way, pretty much coasting. I had taken the boat out of gear and had come out onto the bow to look. I had the camera in my hand, but was awestruck by a huge killer whale surfacing about twenty-five feet ahead of us. She was so close she looked huge. The whale came up, arched her back really hard right in front of us and dove down. We then recognized what we had been watching, and it made me feel so bad, because we just harassed a mother who was nursing her baby twins. I had never heard of twin killer whales. It had been a long, tiresome day for us, capped off by the bad boat maneuver we did around those whales. We decided to just let the whales go on their way. We went into the bay and anchored.

After the engine had been going for so many hours, and having been in rough water all day, it was great to be anchored there, still and quiet. We went into catatonic mode up on the deck. It was really beautiful; it was not raining for once, and there was still some daylight left. We were sitting out there relaxing on our boat in the wilderness when we heard soft respirations coming from down the bay. The breaths were very small and quick. The sound of mammals breathing was reflecting off a big rock wall farther down the bay.

The animals were coming closer, so we got the binoculars out. We could see a group of something swimming toward us from along the edge of the shore. They came right around the boat. They were harbor porpoises. There must have been fifty adults, with at least twenty-five babies. They were swimming around and under the boat. It was if they were thanking us for scaring away the whales who could eat them.

I didn't feel so bad anymore. The harbor porpoises around our boat would come up and take a quick breath, then would go nuts under the water. They were swimming circles around the anchor chain. They would do this 'ring around' thing - the babies would chase each other and roll over each other and their moms. They were having a great time.

The babies could not sound and stay underwater for very long. They were newborn, and looked like ten pound salmon. They were tiny things, with all different colors and splotches. They swam up by the sandy beach, close in to shore. Their moms would slap their tails on the water, perhaps to keep them out of the shallow water. They swam around our old boat while we relaxed.

Hi Buddy

Patrick Cotten was born on his parents' Rumrunner which had been converted to a private yacht. He built his first boat at the age of seven. He built his first ocean going boat when he was twenty-three, in 1965. A year later he sailed in it to New Zealand, going through three hurricanes - right through the eye of one. Patrick has sailed 80,000 ocean miles. He's built thirty-six boats and designed a hundred of them. He is currently writing his third book about the sea.

The finest whale experience I have had happened in early February 1980 while sailing on *Harmony*. She is a fifty foot long fero-cement ketch weighing forty-three tons which I designed and built. We were about 2,500 miles into the South Pacific from San Diego, about a week or so away from the Marqueses.

Harmony was under full sail. We had 2,000 square feet of sail up: twin head sails on twenty foot poles, top sails, mizzen stay sail - everything up. The self steering was driving: we had not touched the tiller in two weeks other than minor adjustments on the wind vane. We were traveling at about eight knots at the time, throwing a four foot wave at our bow and stern.

It was a bright sunny day, about eighty-five degrees. It was idyllic sailing. I was between chapters in the book I was reading and stood up to scan the horizon. About a mile or so away, directly behind us in our wake, I saw a huge whale blow.

I called to my wife, Dana, to get the camera. Maybe the whale was not as far away as I had thought, but he was many hundreds of yards away when I first saw him. By the time Dana had grabbed the camera and returned, the whale had just passed our bow.

I remember the whale coming by on our starboard side so close to the boat that I looked directly down on him. The quarter deck was about ten feet above the water, so my eye was, perhaps, fourteen feet from the whale. He was a little longer than the boat, between fifty and sixty feet long.

The whale rolled up on his side as he passed by, less than a foot under water, within five feet of the boat. His eye was about the size of a basketball and it was looking straight into mine, I felt we had complete communication: he looked at me, I recognized him; I looked at him, he recognized me. It was a connection, a feeling like I never had before in my life, or since.

After we looked at each other, the whale rolled his head back down into the water and was gone. He had to have been making twenty knots, easily doubling our speed. I was impressed.

Wow!

Elise and Rod DuFour lived aboard their boat in Everett, Washington for five years, then moved to Maui. They now live in Friday Harbor, Washington. Elise works for a boat broker, and Rod Captains and does boats maintenance.

Rod and I had taken our thirty-eight foot sailboat out and anchored in the lee of Camano Island, a little north of Everett, Washington. We took our inflatable dinghy and motored around to Langley for lunch. The wind was not blowing too hard in the passage, so we could easily make the crossing.

As we rounded the Camano Head, we saw another sailboat in the passage about 500 yards away. Through the binoculars, I could see there were Dall's porpoises riding off her bow. I had never seen those beautiful black and white porpoises up close before. They swam for five minutes with the sailboat, then they veered away to join a powerboat going the other direction.

As soon as the people aboard the powerboat saw the porpoises and shut down to watch them, the porpoises swam off and disappeared.

I yelled to Rod to go over and see the porpoises. There was a little six-horse engine on our dinghy, and we were going along at full throttle, very close to the water.

"No," he said in his calm way. "If they are going to come, they'll to come to us. We won't go to them, because that may scare them off." For about five minutes there was absolutely nothing. All of a sudden, there were eight Dall's porpoises all around us, swimming with our dinghy. We could look over the edge and see them underneath us. They would roll on their sides and look up at us. It seemed as if they were smiling.

Two of them would come up together and bump the dinghy, cross under us, jump and cross in midair right in front of our little boat. Then they would come up on the sides and blow spray, and get us all wet. I was screaming at the top of my lungs. My husband looked at me and jokingly asked, "How come you never get this excited with me?"

The porpoises stayed with us until we got about fifty yards from the entrance of Langley Harbor, then they veered off. We tied the boat in and ran up the hill as fast as we could. The porpoises were probably two miles up the passage by the time we got to a good vantage point.

I had wanted to bring the camera, but we decided not to. It was a good thing, because we got soaking wet from the porpoises' spray when they came up to breathe. ✒

Oops!

Scott Fratcher *had done a lot of bicycle traveling before he got involved with boats. He and his wife Allison put together a vessel with built-in welding and sail-repair shops, so they could drive around and maintain other people's yachts. They were in Mexico for seven years, then sailed to Alaska in 1994 where they took jobs working in the tourist trade showing people the Alaskan Inside Passage. Allison is the First Mate of the* Executive Explorer, *and Scott is the Chief Engineer. The boat is the fastest small cruise ship in Southeast Alaska, and spends the majority of her time searching out whales and other wildlife.*

Five channels come together on the way into La Paz, Mexico in Baja California. One comes in from the Sea of Cortez, another comes between two islands. A third comes out of a sandbar and another comes from two other islands. It is usually a good spot for sea life.

One of the areas is about six miles wide and especially active. Big fish chase smaller fish, dolphins chase bigger fish, whales swim by. It is an important feeding site for many animals.

As we motored through, a large fin whale came up next to the boat. He surfaced, rolled over onto his side and looked up at us. Then he dove under. We were moving fairly slowly at the time, about four knots. The whale came back up, fifty or sixty yards off to our starboard side. As he came up, the whale was on a collision course with our boat.

The whale started swimming really fast. He was charging directly at us. Just as the whale got to our boat he dove underneath us. A minute or so later, he surfaced at about the same distance away, charging at the boat again.

Allison ran up to the foredeck and was hanging off the bowsprit. As soon as she did this, the whale changed course. He was aiming right for her.

He repeated this many times. Each time, just before he dove, he would roll over on one side looking at Allison. I was at the back of the boat at the helm steering. The whale was longer than our boat, maybe fifty feet. Each time he surfaced, he got a little bit closer.

I never felt as if he was charging us with aggression or malice, but more like a dog playing with a ball. I kept feeling as if he wanted us to do something. But there was very little we could do. I simply held our course, watched the whale and enjoyed the show.

The whale did this charging behavior at least fifteen times. It went on for quite a while. We were almost through the six mile cut before he quit. On what turned out to be the final charge, the whale came towards us quite fast. As the whale dove he must have misjudged his trajectory, because he ended up head butting the bow of the boat. We have a steel boat, so he did not do anything but push the bow to the side a little bit. When the whale hit the boat, he stopped immediately. Maybe he wanted to get more downwards motion, so he put his tail into the air. There it was, ten feet above us. The whale held it there, then slowly submerged as we went along beside his flukes.

It was scary seeing the monstrous tail flukes. They were fifteen feet across. Only a few feet of air was between the tail and me. Then it was over. We never saw the whale again.

At the time our boat had black bottom paint. A friend of ours also had black bottom paint on his fiberglass boat which was shaped similarly to ours. He told us that as he went through the same area, a fin whale that matched our whale's description came up and started rubbing his back on his boat's keel. The whale did this for about four minutes. We wondered if it was the same whale.

Surfing With Whales

Dawn Patrol

Tom Croley works in sales. He lives on a houseboat in Sausalito. He has always been attracted to the water. Tom has been an active wind surfer since 1986. He has a twenty-seven foot Catalina sailboat. Whenever he gets a chance to get out on the water, he takes it. That is where Tom feels most at home.

Montarra, California is about ten minutes north of Half Moon Bay and fifteen minutes south of San Francisco. My friend Brian, who lives in Montarra, invited me to go surfing with him at the beginning of March 1985. He likes to go out on what he calls 'Dawn Patrol.' Before the first light of day, when the water is the calmest, there is no wind, boats or other surfers. The ocean is all yours.

We had paddled out past the white water, turned around and were sitting on our boards waiting for the first set of waves to come in. We caught a few, paddled back out and were sitting on our boards waiting again. It was a new surfing spot to me. Whenever surfing at a new spot, it's good to know exactly where the hazard zones lie. For example, there are occasionally rocks underneath the water. I wanted to make sure not to surf into rocks.

I looked over to our left and saw water starting to boil over something. I asked Brian about the rocks to the left. He said he had been surfing there for seven years and there were no rocks. Well, what was I seeing?

Fifteen feet away from us, a whale surfaced and blew! We both jumped up onto our boards. We were very startled, and quickly turned our boards around to look at it. Sure enough, there was a forty foot long humpback whale laying on the surface right in front of us. We could not believe it.

The sun was just starting to rise. The light on the foam of the breaking waves made by the surfacing whale was beautiful. We sat there in astonishment wondering what he was doing there. We thought he might be rubbing his belly against the sand on the bottom of the beach break. After about fifteen minutes, we caught some more waves and paddled back out. Sure enough, the whale was still right there. We surfed and cut right in front of him. He never moved. For a good forty minutes he was floating there. We were surfing with this whale! He would move in and out a little bit, occasionally diving, but never more than ten feet from the spot where we waited to catch the waves. It seemed like he enjoyed bobbing with the waves. They were not crashing down on him, as he was just outside the break. The waves were about six feet high.

Since then, Brian has seen other whales. A mother and baby were at the same beach break just laying on the surface, bobbing in the waves while he was surfing. He got within eight feet of them.

It is startling to sit on an eight foot long surf board with a wild animal that large laying in the water next to you. Then I realized that this big, beautiful, docile, intelligent creature was simply floating in the water enjoying the same thing I was. I felt connected to the ocean and what was in the ocean, and to these whales, and watched the sun rise on the 'Dawn Patrol.'

Changed My Life

Dennis Grove is a surfer, artist and educator living in South Africa. He also owns The Whale Shop *in Plentenburg Bay.*

I used to live in San Francisco until I got sick from surfing in the polluted water. I decided to go back home to South Africa and try to do something about the pollution in the oceans.

After returning home I was paddling on my surf board trying to catch a wave when I saw something sticking out of the water. It was a southern right whale, spyhopping.

I paddled over to the whale and it dove underneath me. I could see it really well in the clear water. The whale swam in a circle beneath me, then came up about two feet away. As he dove, his tail rose above me and I touched it with my finger tips. I could feel the whale tense up. I never realized what sensitive creatures they are.

I am a store designer. I met a woman on the beach who had an empty store in the town of Hermanus, a popular whale watching destination in South Africa. I suggested she open a shop for whale items. It became a great success.

Later, we found an old house in Plentenberg Bay where whalers used to live. We set up another store. I painted the inside of the shop in an underwater scene with whales on the walls. We filled the shop with a variety of whale and dolphin related items and played tapes of whale sounds. We got a lot of publicity and people came from far away to see our little shop. This seemed like a good way to educate people about the ocean and the animals that live in it.

We asked local craftspeople to produce dolphins or whales in whatever medium they worked. It created an industry: all of a sudden the dolphin pots were selling better than other designs. Artists realized that dolphins were a marketable subject.

The whole town is starting to change. People are using dolphins and whales in logos for their companies. Images of cetaceans are all over the place. People now come to this town to see and learn about the whales. It was previously known as a party town - now it is changing. This is a way for people to recognize what species of animals are living here and how often the whales come by.

We have sighted not only the southern right whales, but also humpbacks, fin and orca whales, as well as three species of dolphins: common, bottlenose and humpback. Three dolphin pods live around the coast. One has over a thousand animals. Another pod has about two hundred, the third only ten. They are humpback dolphins and are on the endangered list. We surf with them every day.

The first time I was with a whale on my surfboard was the most powerful experience of my life. I was a young surfer cruising around the world, not caring about our environment. Now I have dedicated my life to environmental awareness. Things changed the moment I looked into the eye of that whale.

Since I have lived here I have touched four southern right whales. They swim close to the beach, forty-five to sixty feet out. They lie there and are the most beautiful creatures.

At the moment there is a big controversy because the law in South Africa states that you are not allowed to go within three hundred meters of a whale or dolphin. There are organizations trying to enforce it. We find dolphins with bullet holes in their head and we find dead seals that have been clubbed. To end this we have started the Whale and Dolphin Foundation to promote whale watching and ocean awareness.

The way to make people respect the ocean is to put them in the water where it is not our world. This will let human beings see how dolphins, whales, fish, and everything else whose home is the sea, live in their own environment.

Flotsam

Whale Crier

Michael Marzolla has run the 4-H program for The University of California Cooperative Extension in Santa Barbara County, California since 1983. Michael is involved with marine and aquatic education. He was in the Peace Corps for four years in Central America, and has also worked in Africa.

In Namibia, on the Atlantic side of Africa, there is an area known as the 'Skeleton Coast.' It is called that, not because of wrecked ships and dead crews on the desert, but because it was covered with whale bones. In the 1800s, Yankee whalers would regularly kill whales just offshore and pull them up onto this beach to flense them. They left the bones on the shore. At one time it was completely covered with bones up and down the coast, hence the name. We found some evidence of those events. It is an interesting, although very grim, tidbit of history.

Southern right whales gather at Hermanus, in South Africa, east of Cape Town on the Atlantic Ocean. Humpbacks and other breeds of whales are also seen there. This area was another site of intense whaling activity in the old days.

The water is very deep next to the cliffs along the bay. Whales will come up to the cliffs and rub on them. Often they will spyhop high enough to allow people on the edge of the cliff to touch the their heads and snouts.

The town of Hermanus, a popular tourist destination, funds a Whale Crier. People who sight a whale will call the Crier on his cellular phone to let him know where they saw them: "There is a pod here, or a calf-cow pair there, at such and such a distance from shore." The Crier has a trumpet he makes from bull kelp which he blows to get people's attention. He wears a sandwich board displaying the sighting data. He is also very knowledgeable about whales and he shares this information with the public. The present Crier is a Cape colored man named Peter. When I spoke with him, he was on his way to England to participate in a Town Crier convention. He believed that he would be the only Whale Crier there.

The whales have made South Africa a 'destination.' They were a whaling nation not so long ago. It is a very positive change, and reflects the changing relationship between whales and humans.

Research

Biologics

Al Phillips fished in the ocean as a kid and has always been inter-ested in animals of the sea. This encouraged him to get a degree in oceanography. He was in the Navy for over twenty years, all of it in submarines. Starting off cleaning the heads and washing decks, Al worked himself up to electronics technician on nuclear reactors. He retired as a Lieutenant Commander on Trident subs. Now Al is rearing his teenage children, and makes stained glass art. Marine mammals are a common theme in his work.

In the ocean, both whales and submarines spend ninety per cent of their time submerged, so their senses are acoustically oriented. For a submarine, the acoustic world is *the* world. The visual world is sec-ondary. A submarine does not go to the surface unless it has to.

One of the things about the acoustic world, which applies to both whales and submarines, is the lower the frequency of a sound, the fur-ther it travels in the ocean. Because of the mechanics of atom interac-tion in the water, low frequency sounds have less energy loss than high frequency sounds.

The submarine world has noticed over the last hundred years that the volume of noises in the low frequency range has increased enor-mously, from a rumble to a roar. That roar is the immense amount of seaborne traffic on the surface by merchant marine vessels. There are more and more big ships rumbling with three, four, or five bladed pro-pellers thrashing next to the surface generating a low frequency which penetrates the ocean very well, and gets entrained in what is called the sound channel.

The sound channel is an area within the ocean where the density and temperature of the water is such that, as the water goes deeper, it gets cooler and more dense. It quits getting cooler at some point, but it continues to get more dense, so that sound will be reflected by that denser water layer towards the surface. As sound goes towards the sur-face, it gets reflected back down by upper layers of warm water.

There are areas in the ocean which will entrap and then entrain low frequency sounds. Some low frequency sounds, if they are repetitious enough, can be heard over enormous distances - thousands of miles, perhaps further.

In my spare time on submarines, I postulated that many of the whales which project low frequency sounds could have heard each other over hundreds, if not thousands, of miles. It may have been possible, in the right circumstances, that they could be heard from ocean to ocean. So, a humpback whale in the Hawaiian archipelago sending out noises may have been talking to his buddies in the Gulf of Alaska.

The whale's world has suddenly become fogged up. Their acoustic world, because of the increased background noise, and their ability to discern specific signals which are very faint, is being lost.

The ocean is full of old sounds. Every sea mount that you see on the charts is a moving, growing, top of a volcano. The lava down there is not hot enough to boil the water. You can expose red-hot lava to sea water and not cause it to boil at the bottom of the ocean, but what it does do is rumble. I could tell where the sea mounts were because I could hear them.

And, you could hear whales. You could also hear storms on the surface. The ocean is filled with all sorts of higher frequency biologic and non-biological activities which cause acoustic occurrences.

From time to time, our submarines would pass whales. As far as I could tell, there were sperm whales spaced along the continental slopes in every ocean, making sounds we picked up. Sperm whales echo locate differently than the other whales: theirs' sound like a carpenter hitting a sheet of plywood with a hammer.

Every once in a while one of the whales would pick up the pace, and then quit. I speculated, without any actual observation, that one of them had sensed something. He was down there echo locating for prey, detected something and picked up the speed. Then he got involved and quit echo locating, because he was in close proximity, or he had his mouth full.

The Navy was not much interested in biological activity. They wanted to be able to discern what was biologics and what was mechanics. So we made that determination and the biologics were shunted aside.

A part of the sonar technicians' listening certification is to be able to determine biologics from mechanical man-made sounds. But we were unable to select what biologics went with which animal. It could be fish or mammal noise.

The sonar room was off limits to the rest of the crew because of the sensitivity of its technology. The crew did not get involved in sonar, and the sub's officers were too caught up with war game exercises. I was a sonar officer for many years and that was one of the reasons I got involved with whales. I also had a personal interest.

One time when the sonar supervisor picked up an unknown sound the Captain ordered 'silent running' and I was called in to listen. We were in the more northern latitudes and had new sonar gear aboard.

We were able to utilize a number of filtering systems to get rid of many miscellaneous oceanic noises. By the time we fine tuned everything, there was a sound that came from the ocean which went 'thump-thump, thump-thump,' like the frequency of a slow, large human heart.

Our speculation was that this was a baleen whale. We were able to triangulate it at about five miles away. Sonar was sensitive enough to pick up whale heart at five miles. Everyone relaxed and we all breathed a bit easier when we declared what we were listening to was the heartbeat of a whale.

The sound we were hearing had absolutely no mechanical characteristics. Any man made system in the ocean has to be supported by pumps and electronics which always send out specific frequencies that can be determined. While a heart is a pump, it does not have the frequencies of electrical gear. A heart is a biologic sound.

When our 16,000-ton submarine pushed through the ocean, the sea above us lifted up as we went by. We were huge. Our three dimensional bow wake was picked up very well by marine animals. Even at a depth of hundreds of feet, screaming and squealing dolphins would swim down to ride our bow wake, just like the way they rode bow wakes of boats on the surface.

We were in the Caribbean many a time on the surface. I would call up, "Ahead. Go to twelve knots." It would be like a movie - John Wayne would be riding into the valley. He'd look up on his left shoulder, and along the ridge all these Indians would show up. He'd look up on his right shoulder, and along that ridge, more Indians would show up. You go to twelve knots in a big submarine, and off on the right horizon: splash! splash! splash! And off on the left: splash! splash! splash! The dolphins sensed the submarine pick up or slow down to the speed they liked, and porpoised as fast as they could to play with us. We would have a hundred dolphins riding in our bow wake!

The vocalizations I heard dolphins make sounded more like *Star Wars* and electric synthesizer music than any recorded dolphin squeaks and squeals I've heard. Their vocalizations were much more flavorful, it's like spices versus salt. If you consider *Flipper* salt, these wonderful ZzzzUuuuSssss...POP! WeeeeLeee...OOP! Cheeep...Its...BIP! clicks, snaps and strange whistlings were great acoustic spices.

Our sonar was set up to scan great distances, so we were not refining or tracking who was coming at us close by. But you could tell when dolphins got next to the submarine because the decibels would go up by fifty. When dolphins were riding our bow wave and we were submerged, you could hear them through the hull of the vessel. Everyone in the boat could hear them.

In general, marine mammals were not a topic of much interest amongst submariners. Our lives were full, we worked twenty to twenty-two hours a day just trying to keep up.

Our interactions with whales and dolphins were rare and wonderful highlights which I enjoyed. ⬐

Science

John Calambokidas and his wife Gretchen have worked together for fifteen years. They met while doing marine mammal research. Their son is also getting involved in their work. Gretchen and John have recently published a book titled Blue Whales.

We started Cascadia Research Collective a year after graduating from The Evergreen State College in Olympia, Washington. All of the founders were graduates from Evergreen, none had advanced academic degrees. A number of us had studied marine mammals in college. Our first projects were with the National Marine Fisheries Service.

We began our humpback and blue whale projects in 1986, working with Ken Balcomb off California. Beginning in the early nineties, we shifted to looking at the population size off the entire west coast through photographic identification. One of the dominant objectives we had was assessing population size and movement patterns. We have built a long term database of humpback, gray and blue whale ID photographs. We now have over a thousand blue whales identified by their natural markings.

We also keep sighting locations in the database, and keep records of individual whales. The longest individual on record has been identified for twenty years.

We identify two to three hundred animals each year and match them to our catalogue. The blue whale photographs reveal that the first good estimate of the California population is two thousand, quite a bit more than anyone thought existed in the whole North Pacific.

We still have photo ID'd only half of the population. Each year we are building on that, finding a high proportion of new animals.

It turns out the population of humpbacks is smaller than of blue whales. There are about seven hundred humpbacks off California; we have almost all of them identified. On average, we photograph three or four hundred humpback whales each year.

We have also been doing work with humpbacks in Costa Rica. We are finding that most of the humpbacks seen there in the winter feed off California in the summer. We recognize most of the whales we see in Costa Rica.

The first time we experienced 'friendly' whale behavior was in 1992. I was alone in a sixteen foot inflatable in Santa Barbara Channel. Two adult humpbacks, fifty feet long, swam up and lay motionless under my boat. They spyhopped beside the boat. Then one of the whales began to touch the boat's air-filled rubber sides very gently with the tip of its fifteen foot long, two thousand pound pectoral fin. As the fin came closer, I was not sure whether I should stay and watch or get away from the whale.

The humpback was tentative at first, as if it were unsure of what would happen when it made contact with the boat. After learning that the object of its attention was not only soft, but would move across the top of the water, the whale lay on its back with its pectoral fins on either side of the boat and started pushing it in circles. The whale then lifted the boat up in the air about two feet on its belly. The second whale soon joined the first at playing with the inflatable - and me!

The whales' great control of their bodies was startling. When they first got close to the boat and touched it, I was nervous they might make contact with the boat by accident. However, they did not make any contact until it was deliberate. Their behavior was very controlled.

One thing puzzled me. I photographed both whales and looked for them in the database. They had never been seen before in our research, and have never been seen since. On average, each whale we identify has been seen about ten times. It is very unusual to have a whale that is only seen once. To have two whales engaged in this friendly behavior that have never been seen before or since is very odd.

Very friendly humpback   *Photo: John Calambokidas*

There has been a dramatic increase in friendly encounters in the last decade. We have been curious about the cause. We are looking at the connections between animals that engage in this behavior, and how it spreads through a population. Many individuals repeat interactions during a year. In several cases the same whales engaged in this friendly behavior in successive years.

When we observe some whales standing off, we can watch how behavior spreads through the population. One or two animals engage in friendly interactions, and others are exposed to that behavior.

Although awed by the encounter in the field, as scientists we have to see what we can learn about this behavior. We have noticed some increase in blue whales' friendly interactions, but it is a fraction of the humpbacks' rate. We try to set up a rigid set of conditions to define friendly encounters, making sure we are not incorrectly considering cetacean behavior friendly.

We start with the premise that what we do disturbs whales. We want to make sure that what we do is justified, even if this is a disturbance. We try to be cautious about these friendly behaviors - is it really a healthy thing? Maybe not. Maybe it is going to get whales in trouble and injured in the long run. We are concerned about their evolving relationship with humans. It is nice to think whales love us and they are doing all this out of interest, but we may be wrong on that.

If there is a potential risk to the whales from our research, we want to make sure the findings are worthwhile. With the explosion of whale watching, it is easy to envision a situation where animals are harmed by the interest people have in them, no matter how well-intentioned.

Originally, photographic identification was intended to provide information in a way that did not harm animals. I have come to accept that even this is potentially invasive.

We decided to engage in biopsying, taking samples of skin for genetic analysis. Some people find these techniques invasive. But only through biopsies have the high toxic levels in our local orca population become known.

Many oceanographers and other biologists feel that all creatures are worthy of the attention cetaceans receive. I agree. Humans see whales as a metaphor, something that captures our imagination and serves to represent protecting the marine environment as a whole.

I want to see species and the environment protected, as a priority over saving individual animals. Instances exist where millions of dollars are spent to save an individual animal. Sometimes there is incredibly irony. A great deal of money was spent trying to save three gray whales which were trapped in the ice near Barrow, Alaska - even though gray whales were still being hunted! You have to laugh and wonder, if that made any economic sense.

You think about situations like the vaquita in the Sea of Cortez, a harbor porpoise that is down to just a couple of hundred animals and in danger of extinction within the next ten or twenty years, largely because they get entangled in fish nets. The fishery is not all that valuable. With the million dollars spent trying to save one whale, you could save an entire species by buying out the fishermen that are entangling vaquitas.

I share people's fascination with whales. Obviously they are intelligent, curious, and long-lived. Certainly many of the animals that are alive today experienced whaling.

As time passes, possibilities for a curious animal to learn new behavior increase. Thirty years ago a curious whale was a dead whale. There was a very powerful disincentive against friendly behavior in whales for a long time. It may take a while for it to return again.

Communication

Captives

Robert Swanson had a twenty year career in the Navy, where he flew in typhoons, worked on an aircraft carrier flight deck, and recovered two Apollo capsules. When Robert retired from the Navy, he spent six years in law enforcement. After that, he spent about twenty-five years in maintenance management in a manufacturing environment. Then Robert retired and went Elderhosteling.

While I was in the Navy, I served in Viet Nam on an aircraft carrier. One of my duties was to launch and recover aircraft. I had the misfortune one morning in 1965 to launch our Carrier Air Group Commander Stockdale. He was shot down and captured, and spent seven-and-a-half years in the 'Hanoi Hilton' in North Viet Nam.

Just a few months later I launched our Squadron Commanding Officer Jenkins. He was also shot down and captured, and also spent seven-and-a-half years in the same prison.

They were not released until 1973, the year I retired from the Navy. I knew it was not my fault, but I was one of the last of their countrymen to talk to them before they were captured. It has bothered me to this day, even though both men survived and are safe and sound with their families. The experience left me with strong feelings about people and animals being locked up.

In the sixties and seventies, a big craze seemed to come over the country for capturing dolphins and whales. Putting them on display, and running them through their paces like a bunch of trained monkeys, did not seem a humane treatment of animals to me.

I've done some reading and I know that the whale family are thinking creatures. They have powers superior to ours, as far as communication over distance and intelligence. I believe they are telepathic.

A few years ago some of my family was visiting. It was long after the two pilots had been released and safely returned home. We happened to be at the Minnesota Zoo with our grandkids. One of the displays there is a dolphin tank where they do their 'tricks' and get fed. The rest of the time the dolphins just swim around.

I did not want to watch the dolphins, but the grandkids begged, and I agreed. I was watching the bubbles from the dolphins' leaps and their activities from below through the large windows. Everything got quiet so I figured the show was over. All of a sudden, I was thinking about Stockdale and Jenkins, and about people being locked up. I was thinking about the hopelessness of a situation like that. I leaned against the glass staring into the water, letting my thoughts drift.

Then I thought: "You poor dolphins. What in Hell did you do to deserve this?" All of a sudden, I had a feeling there was somebody telling me something. It was not a message of any kind. I felt as if there was somebody in a situation that was hopeless or helpless.

Just at that time, one of the dolphins swam up to the window and looked me right in the eye, and held that eye contact. Then he turned and swam away and the feeling left me. I believe he was telling me, "Yeah. I know what you are thinking. Yes, you are right! I do not want to be here." It was a strong feeling that came over me, a feeling that led me to tears.

I believe I understood the message behind my feeling. Everyone thinks that dolphins are happy because they look like they are smiling, but that's just a physical characteristic. It is just the way their face looks.

I do not know if it was simply coincidence that I was having those thoughts about the pilots in prison when the dolphin swam up and we looked at each other. Or, that the feeling left when he swam away. I like to think it was more than that.

Voice of the Whales

Mary Getten has studied and worked with marine mammals since 1987. She has been a naturalist on whale watching boats in the San Juan Islands of Washington State and in Maui, Hawaii since 1990. Mary is a coordinator of the Marine Mammal Stranding Network, the Islands Oil Spill Association, and is a staff member at Wolf Hollow Wildlife Rehabilitation Center. She is also a telepathic animal communicator with a professional practice on Orcas Island, Washington. She gives How to Communicate with Animals *workshops around the country. Mary is the author of* The Orca Pocket Guide. *Her next book will be,* Voice of the Whales: Conversations with an Orca Elder.

My animal consultations are mainly with people who have various pet problems: the dog barks too much, the cat won't eat, the turtle is acting lethargic. I communicate with the animal telepathically and find out what is going on from their viewpoint. Then I relay the information to their person and together we try to find a solution.

Telepathic communication is an innate ability which most of us have forgotten. Fortunately, it can be regained. I began studying this skill in 1988. It's much like learning a foreign language and involves a lot of practice until you become better at it.

Telepathic communication comes to the receiver in many forms: words, pictures, physical or emotional feelings and even through an intuitive sense of 'knowing.' Each person receives in various ways at different times depending on the animal, although some people are strongest in one area.

Animal consulting is very rewarding when I am able to comprehend pets from their viewpoint and help them come to a better understanding with their person. Although it is not effective in every case, it's great when I can help with a decision about euthanasia, or change a behavior pattern, or find lost animals.

Once I had a call about an iguana who had escaped from her cage. After looking everywhere on their property with no success, the people called me. It was getting dark and they were frantic. I mentally tuned into the iguana and found that she was still in the backyard. Through the iguana's eyes I could see the picnic table and the back of the house. The picture I got was rather blurry. It seemed like there were leaves overhead, so I suggested that the iguana was in the blackberry bushes in the yard. About half an hour later the woman called to say they had found the iguana. The animal had climbed up into an apple tree and was falling asleep. Her eyes were half closed when they found her, which is why I was seeing everything so blurry. I was right about the leaves, but they were on an apple tree, not on blackberry bushes.

Since 1990, I've been a naturalist on a whale watch boat in Friday Harbor, Washington, educating passengers about the wildlife of this area. Over the years I have had many incredible encounters with the resident orcas that frequent these waters in the summer.

I did not combine these two occupations until 1995, when my love for the whales, and curiosity, overcame me. Over the years I had developed a relationship with *Granny*, the leader of J pod. I always looked for her on our trips and yelled, "Hey *Granny!*" when she swam by.

I enjoyed these interactions, but I wanted to know more about her life. My view of her world was limited to the brief intervals *Granny* spent at the surface, only about three minutes an hour, or five percent of the time. I wanted to know about the other ninety-five percent of her life. So I decided to contact *Granny* telepathically.

I was nervous about approaching such an impressive and magnificent being, but gradually my desire to learn about her overcame my fear. I went to the west side of San Juan Island and sat on the rocks by Lime Kiln Lighthouse. When the whales swam by, I mentally introduced myself and started communicating in my mind with *Granny*.

She was very willing to talk. *Granny* recognized me as "the blonde woman who yells at her from the *Western Prince*." I was thrilled! We continued to talk after that. Occasionally, I was given information which was contrary to scientific belief. I found this quite confusing. I was not sure if I was hearing *Granny* wrong, or if the researchers were incorrect. I did not think I could talk to whale researchers about these discrepancies, because telepathic communication is generally regarded with skepticism by the scientific community. So I kept the talks and information to myself.

In 1996, Raphaela Pope, an animal communicator I had met at an interspecies counselor course, came to visit. I took her out whale watching and asked her to verify a few things with *Granny*. I wanted confirmation on the information I was getting. She was happy to oblige and in the process also fell in love with the whales.

I proposed that Raphaela and I work together to investigate the lives of orcas. She was intrigued with the idea, but was concerned that her lack of knowledge about whales would be a problem. I thought the contrary. Since she had absolutely no preconceived ideas about the whales, she would not interfere with clear communication. I knew a lot about their lives and could interpret things that Raphaela might not understand. I felt we were the perfect combination for this work.

We asked *Granny* if she would be willing to talk to us and answer questions on a regular basis. The whale was delighted and eager to communicate with us. Raphaela and I took turns being the communicator while the other one acted as an interviewer. It was easier to stay focused this way. If we were talking about a subject that I felt I had a particular bias or opinion on, Raphaela would do the communicating so I could ask the questions. Sometimes my knowledge was helpful in the communicator role, so we traded positions frequently.

We had some amazing moments, such as the time Raphaela said, "I don't know what *Granny* is showing me, but I see two lines of whales facing each other. It looks like they are on a football field at the kick off." She went on to describe an entire greeting ceremony in minute detail, but had no ideas what she was seeing. If I hadn't been working with her, she wouldn't have understood what *Granny* was showing her. But I knew, and this experience convinced me without a doubt that we were receiving *Granny* clearly.

A greeting ceremony is a very rare and special ritual performed by the local orcas. In nine years on the water, I have only seen one complete greeting ceremony. It was between J and K pods at Turn Point on Stuart Island. After the whales lined up facing each other, there was complete silence and no movement. Then suddenly both lines advanced at top speed. When they met, the whales rubbed and rolled on each other. The air was filled with their squeaks and squeals, and water flew everywhere. The pandemonium lasted for about ten minutes, and then the whales split into small groups and traveled north together.

Often it was difficult to know the 'right' questions to ask *Granny*, since the orca's world is so different from ours. Over the years, we have questioned *Granny* and her family about every facet of their lives: their physical bodies, sex, social interactions, feeding, territory, spirituality, problems, children, whales in captivity, and their interactions with humans.

One thing that surprised us was the amount of information *Granny* knew about the everyday lives of humans. We asked her how this was possible and she replied: "We get information in many ways. Do you know how many thousands of ships have plied these waters in my lifetime? Do you know how many conversations we have listened to with eager interest? Do you know how many radio broadcasts I have heard? Besides, as you well know, we are very capable of telepathic communication.

"We receive thought pictures from the people who come to see us and this helps us learn about your world. People are not very focused with their thoughts. They see us, become excited and send messages of love or ask us to do things - always they want us to do things. Then images of a movie they watched the night before, or a friend, pops into their minds and we continue to get those pictures. They do not stay focused, so we are constantly picking up information about their world."

Be careful what you think in the presence of whales. They are tuned into your thoughts and receive everything.

We also interviewed four captive whales for their views on life and hopes for the future. Raphaela and I went to California to meet *Yaka* and *Vigga* at Marine World Africa USA, and also to Newport, Oregon to see *Keiko*. We also interviewed *Lolita* long distance, without the trip to Miami.

One common thing each of these captive whales told us was: "More Fish! Bigger Fish!" They all said they were hungry and could hardly feel the small dead fish they are fed going down their throats. Raphaela and I now have close relationships with many orcas. We have hundreds of pages of dialogue which we have decided to turn into a book which will tell the whales' story from their perspective.

One day we asked *Granny* if there was something humans can do to help the whales. Without hesitation she replied: "There are two things that people can do to help: one is to leave us alone. We do not need to be managed. We are entirely capable of managing ourselves and did so quite beautifully long before the creation and evolution of human beings. The other is to love, admire, and respect whales as fellow inhabitants of our Earth and we will extend that love and respect to you."

I feel very privileged to have had the opportunity to spend so much time with these orcas in their world. When I am working as a naturalist, I do not ask the whales to come to me, but sometimes fun and unusual things happen. On a trip last summer, J pod was swimming right toward the *Western Prince*, so I went out onto the deck. When I saw *Granny* I yelled my usual, "Hey *Granny*!" She lifted her tail flukes and slapped the surface.

Immediately I yelled at her son, "Hey *Ruffles*!" and he lifted his tail flukes and also slapped the surface. All of the guests on the boat turned around and asked how I did that. I just shrugged, smiled innocently and ran back to the wheelhouse.

The whales know me, and sometimes they acknowledge me in this way, but I never ask them for favors.

When I am working as a naturalist, my job is to educate people about orcas and the wildlife of this area. In my free time, I conduct my own research into their lives.

Interspecies Communication

Jim Nollman is founder and executive director of Interspecies Communication. He is the author of Dolphin Dreamtime; Spiritual Ecology; Why We Garden; *and* The Charged Border, Where Whales and Humans Meet. *His album* Orcas' Greatest Hits *features live music with wild killer whales. Jim and his family live on San Juan Island, Washington.*

I am not a scientist, I am a musician with a passion for conceptual art which led to a life of interspecies communication. An early example of my conceptual art was a radio broadcast recorded with three hundred turkeys entitled, *Music to Eat Thanksgiving Dinner By.*

Making recordings with wolves taught me that animals can recognize musical scales as well as human beings can. The wolves would stop singing if I got off pitch.

I also made music with kangaroo rats. Their nests are like giant steel drums - wherever they thump has a different tone. Another kangaroo rat five hundred yards out in the desert will start thumping back.

Because of the power we give to whales and dolphins, I started making music with them. I went to Hawaii, and brought two instruments that would float. One, a water phone, was made from a salad bowl, a pizza plate and a vacuum cleaner tube, all welded together. It vibrated when rubbed or played with a cello bow. The other instrument was a wooden drum. Every time dolphins came into the bay, I would swim out and greet them with music. The dolphins swam up to me. They were fearless.

Whenever I was making music for the dolphins, crowds of people came to the beach to check it out. Spinner dolphins would start jumping six feet into the air while people clapped and yelled. The dolphins seemed to get energy from them. It is understandable how these animals can be trained to work in an oceanarium.

Greenpeace had a project in Japan to stop the killing of dolphins at Iki Island. Since they had seen an article about my work with wolves and dolphins, they hired me to attract dolphins for a media event. Armies of media came to see dolphins, but not one dolphin came. They were freaked out by the crowds waiting to see and record them. The dolphins were also wary because of previous encounters where their relatives had been killed or captured.

Jim Nollman playing music with orca   Photo: Betty Didcoct

In 1976, I started playing music with orcas on a fifty-foot boat in Johnstone Strait, British Columbia. We had sound systems for doing real time communication, transmission and reception from the water.

After fourteen years I stopped this work when whale watching made it impossible for me to acoustically interact with the whales. From dawn to dusk there were boats around the whales. It was never quiet enough. It was like having a bulldozer in a recording studio. I also felt many of the Canadian whale watching operators did not like hearing guitar sounds through their hydrophones.

I decided to stop working with whales because they were getting mythologized. There was too much 'stuff' around them. People were starting to write me letters about channeling. Even though I never considered myself a 'New Ager,' I understand how I could be interpreted that way. I can appreciate mysticism, but am not interested in promoting it.

I figured there were enough people working with whales. As an artist I wanted to be on the edge, and suddenly, whales and dolphins were mainstream.

As I was trying to stop working with whales, I was invited to Okinawa to play music with an overtone singer who had studied in Outer Mongolia. He could produce two notes with his voice, and could throw one of the voices above his head. The voice coming out of his throat was low and guttural, but the harmonic structure that came out was high-pitched like a whistle.

We worked together for three days. We sang and played music to humpback whales. A mother and calf were near the boat and one of them began to sing their haunting 'song.' The whale sang with us for forty-five minutes. What was strange is most researchers believe only male humpbacks sing. We felt the whale related to us music to music.

I wonder what it is about whales that is such a special thrill to people. Perhaps whales are celebrities and we give them more power than they deserve. They are the Elvis Presleys of the animal world. Or, maybe they actually have some power we can feel. Scientists do not pay any attention to what can't be analyzed. However, the once-distinct lines between scientists, environmentalists and mystics now seem to be softening.

Historically, many cultures have given serious power to dolphins, porpoises, and whales. I believe cetaceans have some unknown, meaningful connection to human hearts and minds. ◁

Party Time

Urmas Kaldveer has been teaching environmental science and concepts of biology for twenty years. Urmas' story Center Yourself *is on page 26.*

Pelagikos, the nonprofit research organization I am involved with, was conducting a class for Mendocino Community College called, *Whale and Dolphin Ecology of the Channel Islands,* aboard *Dariabar,* our 84-foot steel Alden schooner.

We were engaged in sighting whales for identification, behavior, etc. There were hydrophones and tape recorders on board so we could document sounds. Most of the students never had 'The Whale Experience,' the recognition that something happens to you when are in the presence of whales. While it is difficult to describe, to me it is an overpower feeling of intelligence combined with massive gentleness. Certainly the first experience I had with a whale overwhelmed me. Many people feel this way.

During the summer in the Channel Islands, there are as many as two thousand blue whales, probably the largest congregation in the world. We had designated a spot between Santa Rosa and Santa Cruz Islands as 'whale city,' because the previous times we sailed there we had great luck in engaging with a large number of whales. The term 'engaging' is used to convey that we were not simply documenting a species, but engaging in a mutual appreciation.

One of the professors who was with us as a guest speaker was Elizabet Satouris. She had written a book called *The Human Journey, From Chaos To Cosmos*. She had just returned from Peru where she had been under the tutelage of an Inca Shaman. Elizabet asked him what should be done among the whales. He told her to make a party out of it, to have a playful, joyous, attitude within our hearts and souls.

We were in a good place. Without binoculars we could see dozens if not hundreds of humpback and blue whales traveling in various directions. Everybody was excited because there we so many whales, and it was such a beautiful day for a party. People were all over the boat. We had the hydrophones turned up on amplified speakers so we could hear the vocalizations of two different kinds of whales together on deck: the songs of the humpbacks and the occasional, deep 'haruumphfff' of the blue whales.

We were drifting, surrounded by whales. Elizabet had brought along an Australian didgery-doo. We also had shamanic drums, so we decided to play some music for the whales. Elizabet took the didgery-doo below and placed it against the hull of the boat and began playing. It was her idea that the sounds of the instrument would be transmitted through the steel hull into the water, where the whales would hear it.

Through the hydrophones it seemed as though the blue whales were responding to the sounds she made. Elizabet would play a couple of notes and almost identical notes would come back to us from the whales. A great joy was beginning to develop, a feeling that something special was happening. There was a connection being made, and both sides of the connection were cognizant of it. It was a clear example of interspecies communication. We felt the whales were picking up on our joy of being in their presence.

As Elizabet continued to play, the blue whales began to come in closer. A group of three whales, one of them a calf, was traveling at a rapid speed out of the Channel. When they heard the didgery-doo they made a ninety degree turn, and came swiftly towards the boat. Elizabet came up and played to them on the deck, pressing the instrument against the rail of the boat. Pretty soon a group of ten or twelve blue whales was heading from all directions towards *Dariabar.* Seven of them swam head to tail in a circle around us. They were so close that when they came up and blew, we were showered by their spray. Some of their blows were going up fifteen or twenty feet in the air.

The seven whales seemed to be playing a game around the boat: they would dive underneath the bow and come up on the other side. Then they would swim down that side, dive under the stern, surface on the other side, and swim forward to the bow and repeat the pattern. Their movement of water created a vortex with the boat in the center. Although it wasn't dangerous, the boat began to turn within this circular current. The whales stayed with us for at least an hour. Both humpbacks and gray whales are much more prone to have this kind of interaction with people than are the more isolated blue whales.

Interestingly, some of the Native American people in Northern California who have had a long history of association with whales think of the blue whales as the 'elders' of the whale community. They are the 'old ones,' the 'sages,' or 'keepers of the wisdom' of the whales.

It seemed as though the message of the Inca Shaman had gotten through to us, and somehow the whales understood. This was a moment where those barriers that might exist between species were allowed to drop entirely.

Keep Playing

Azuriel Mayo has been Captain on whale watching boats since 1992. He was born around the Columbia River and grew up in Oregon. In 1978 he moved to Bellingham. It was there that Azuriel started his career working on the water. He worked five years on tug boats, then took over the oil spill skimming program for another five years. He also drove the ferry boat from Bellingham to Friday Harbor. Now Azuriel has his own boat Heart's Desire, *and runs Whale Spirit Adventures based on Orcas Island, Washington. He also creates whimsical ceramic figures.*

In 1995, I started playing the flute for whales. I love playing the flute, and I was curious to see if whales would show any interest or response. I found they did.

Azuriel playing the flute for Taku   Photo: Peter Fromm

At first, they would slightly change course to come closer to the boat as they were swimming. I had a baby come up and stay in a continuous spyhop position, rocking his body back and forth, listening as I played. His mother swam up to the boat and looked at me.

One day, *Taku* and his mother, *Lummi*, in K pod, were swimming toward the boat. The engine was off and we were drifting. The whales could easily choose where they wanted to go. I asked the two whales, with my mind and heart, if they wanted to hear music. If they did not want to hear it, I did not want to bother them. "Give me a sign. Because of my love for you, I do not want to add more noise to your environment that is displeasing."

Taku came up to the surface, took a deep dive and went underneath the boat. *Lummi* surfaced in front of the boat. Six people were standing on the bow. She was right below their feet. I was up on the flying bridge playing the flute.

The whale lay on the surface in front of the stopped boat while I continued to play. She slapped her tail flukes slowly on the water five times. It was like applause!

I experienced an overwhelming warmth in my heart. I was amazed that I could still play the flute during that time. When *Lummi* was done slapping her tail, she lay on the surface a little longer, then dove and swam away. I felt tremendously honored that I had been recognized by a superior, loving being. Even now, I can still remember that incredible love feeling.

Death and Dying

Sacrifice

__Don Marshall__ grew up in Chicago during the Al Capone days. He rode freights during the depression, and served with the Marine Corps in World War II. For twenty years Don was a Los Angeles police officer. He has owned a gold mine in the High Sierras, a junk yard, a government surplus store, and several bars. Don has written five books. He teaches history at Elderhostel classes.

The *Corona* was a propellor driven steamship which weighed fourteen-hundred and ninety-two tons. She was built in 1888 by Neffy and Levy in Philadelphia, to replace the loss of the *Encon*, another ship that was working the coast. The *Corona* travelled back and forth to Alaska in the 1898 gold rush.

In 1888, when she was still brand new, the *Corona* ran into Lewis Island in the Lynn Canal. The ship got off the rocks but had a big hole punched in her hull. With the ship sitting dead in the water, the crew put collision mats over the side to cover the hole, but that did not have much effect on slowing the water coming in. Nor did the pumps. There were a lot of people aboard and the ship was sinking. Because the *Corona* was going down so fast, the Captain was about issue the 'abandon ship' order.

All of a sudden, the pumps started to catch up and the inrush of water stopped. Pretty soon, the pumps got enough water out that the *Corona* was in a safe position again. They headed immediately for dry dock in Seattle.

Several days later, when the ship was in the dry dock, a large, quite dead pilot whale was found, his head stuck into the hole the rocks made in the hull. The pilot whale had stopped the water from sinking the *Corona*! Since the ship had been totally stopped with tons of water rushing aboard, and that flood quit so quickly, it was thought the pilot whale intentionally swam at full speed into the hole in the ship. From the way he was positioned, it was considered highly unlikely that the whale would have been sucked head first into the hole by the strength of the flowing water. The pilot whale's swimming ability would have kept him out of danger. At the shipyard, they did not have any whaling tools or cutting instruments, so they had to chop the unfortunate whale out with an axe.

There was an article in the *Washington Post Standard* newspaper about the ship and her passengers being saved by the pilot whale's sacrifice. The event was also mentioned in Wright's *History of the Northwest Coast.*

The *Corona* ran until March 1907, when she wrecked in Humboldt Bay.

A Strong Memory

Jack Helsell, and his wife Jan, live on Orcas Island, Washington, where they have a small farm with Jersey cows and Clydesdale horses. Jack also runs a sawmill.

John Bertoncinni served as the skipper on the yawl *Westward Ho* from 1938-1941. John must have been about 70 years old then. His job was to take groups of young adults on sailing trips in the San Juan Islands during the summer. He maintained and lived on the boat during the winter. He had been hired to do this by Ruth Brown of Four Winds Camp, on Orcas Island.

In the winter, the *Westward Ho* was moored in Lake Washington, in Seattle, between Hunt's and Yarrow Points. While I was in high school, and living nearby, I used to row out to the boat almost every night. I visited with John and watched his progress on a model of a four masted bark. John made the model for Ruth Brown and told her later that the main reason he finished it was that he did not want to disappoint me. Ruth gave me model, and I still have it.

John had served on whaling ships in the Arctic for much of his life, working his way up to Captain. In Arthur James Allen's book, *A Whaler And Trader In The Arctic*, there is not only a photograph and stories about John, but also a painting by John of whaling ships wintering at Herschel Island. Both the photo and painting are in the San Francisco Maritime Museum.

John once told me the only way whalers could get the stinking whale oil out of their clothes was to soak them in a barrel of urine, which the crew contributed. After soaking for a day, the clothes were dragged in the water behind the ship to rinse.

John's most memorable story did not have much humor in it. John's boat was near another whale boat which had struck a whale with a harpoon and was alongside the dying animal. The whale was likely a bowhead, as that was primarily what was hunted in the Arctic at that time. In its final death throes, the whale brought his tail fluke down directly on top of the boat steerer, who was standing up at the stern of the boat. The man was killed instantly, his head driven into his body by the force of the whale's tail. The man's eyes, still wide open, were staring lifelessly out at the world from just above his collar bones.

Many whalers died when their boats were smashed by the animals they were hunting. It was a dangerous way to earn a living. ◁

Beluga Hunt

Jim Justice is a doctor who worked with the Tlingit people in organizing health councils and village health programs. Jim's story Watcha Doin? *is on page 2.*

In 1961, I was living at Kotzebue, Alaska just north of the Arctic Circle. I had bought a Chris Craft cabin boat, a kit boat that a school teacher had made. It had twin thirty-five horsepower outboards. When whaling season arrived, and I heard about it, I asked a group of native people if they would like to come with me, fitting out the boat.

The native people have a system where every seat in the umiak they use to hunt whales is assigned based on tradition. The person in each seat has a job to do: handling floats, coiling line, spotting a whale, throwing a harpoon, etc. This was assigned on a hereditary basis, father to son, through the generations.

The seating arrangement on my boat did not fit any tradition. I was able to get a crew together of people who, supposedly, knew something. But none of the traditional people were with me because they were all in their own boats. I had a group of people who had missed out learning traditional ways. They were either x-ray technicians working at the hospital, or people who had been in the hospital for years with tuberculosis, then stabilized and returned home - in short, people who had not grown up whaling.

The hunters in their umiaks and my crew in the Chris Craft went out for two days and one night. We camped on the ice flow and drifted through the night, hoping to spot whales. The ice had broken up enough so now, by mid-June, there were more leads - water channels - than ice. This kept the water very calm. Large ice pans were floating and you had to make sure you did not get between two pans coming together.

We did not see any belugas for quite a while. Finally, we came to an ice pan that had broken off and had some ice hillocks on it. The umiaks pulled up on the ice, while I set an anchor on the ice for my boat. We climbed up on a little hillock and looked out and saw the belugas spouting off in the distance. The whales made a funny noise that you could hear quite a ways away. We watched them come closer.

When the leader gave a signal, we jumped into the boats and went off after the whales. All the umiaks had outboards. Every boat would sight and take after its own whale. Two boats would be on a collision course chasing their whale, not looking at the other boat at all. The umiaks were going very fast as they weighed next to nothing and had fifty or seventy-five horse outboards, roaring like crazy. They missed each other by feet.

I had been practicing with a harpoon for a week or so before the trip. The x-ray technician had a 30-06 rifle at the bow. He fired several shots into the head of the beluga we were following. Then I got up in the bow and successfully stuck a harpoon in it before it sank. I was able to get the harpoon in and pull the release on it, which left the head of the harpoon imbedded in the flesh, with plastic gallon water jugs acting as floats tied to it. Most of the other guys were also using plastic jugs for floats. A very few had the harbor seal skin turned inside out, filled with air, with the neck and flippers sewn up - the traditional float they used to use.

We lashed the dead beluga whale to my boat. Some of the people in other boats got whales, some of them did not. By this time everyone was hungry. To eat, we pulled up on an ice flow again, and anchored everything. They started a fire going on the ice to boil some food. Before we got to eat real food, I found out that as the one who successfully harpooned a whale, I was required to eat a slice of the flipper.

They cut off a slice of beluga flipper and I sat out there on the boat trying to chew the damned thing. It was like trying to chew a Goodyear tire. It would not go down. I did not know what to do. I did not want to embarrass them or myself, so I called their attention, "Say, hey! Is that a spout over there?" As soon as they looked, I put it in my parka. So, I had all this blubber at the end of the day inside my parka. If they knew I did that, they did not let on. I fulfilled my obligation, that was all they were after.

They cooked whale meat stew. It was very hearty, very fatty, very delicious. We were all sipping and chewing it. That was good. All of a sudden, I looked up. Coming at us was another huge piece of pan ice. The Eskimos did not worry, their boats were up on the ice. My boat was not.

I had to stop eating and run like Hell for the boat. I grabbed the anchor and leaped on board, yanked the engines to life and got them in reverse. My crew was all busy eating, so they were not around to help me, and I did not have time to explain to them what was happening. I backed out through the only open water, which was closing fast. I just barely made it out before one ice pan tilted up and cracked on the other. The whale was still lashed to the boat - it slowed me up in getting out of there. That was close!

On the second day, the pan ice had just about given out, and the water was getting very choppy. A storm was coming up. I could not handle the boat with the whale on the side of it. I could not steer and it seemed like we were losing ground. We all decided, finally, that we had to cut the whale loose. It sank and we got home safely. That was the end of my career as a whale hunter, but at least I had an inkling of what these men do to feed their families. ⤙

Feeding Frenzy

Clyde Rice grew up on boats with his family. He has been a commercial fisherman and operated boats for the Scripps Oceanographic Institute for many years. He realized he could not be out at sea all the time and maintain his marriage, so he became a landscape architect, eventually becoming superintendent of parks for a small city. His wife's idea of getting out of the rat race was operating a bed and breakfast on a big boat in Friday Harbor, Washington. Clyde was happy to go along with that.

When I was with The Scripps Oceanographic Institute in the fifties, we had taken on a job for one of the whale watching outfits. We had gone down to two islands that formed a bay. It was about fifty miles north of Cedros Island on the Baja coast. These two islands were the nursery grounds for elephant seals, where the babies were born and raised every year until they could travel. When the young elephant seals were old enough, all the animals would go into the water and start their migration. And every year, waiting for them, was a large pod fifty or sixty killer whales.

As the seals would get into deep enough water to be had, they would be had. A great bull whale would charge out of the water with a big elephant seal in its mouth. The whale would shake its head a little bit and two halves of the seal would fall into the water. While this was going on there was constant screaming, bellowing, roaring, splashing, guts and gore flying every which way.

I was the boatman, and had taken a film and sound crew onto the beach. On my way back, the ship's whistle started blowing five short warning blasts. I didn't know what was going on. Then I noticed that everyone on the ship was pointing at me, waving and shouting and whatnot. I looked astern. Here come a couple of big killer whales right behind me. It scared the pants off me! I knew they didn't attack people, but maybe they would in a feeding frenzy. I didn't want to be the first documented human killed by wild killer whales. So I headed for an outcropping of low rock and beached the boat at full bore up a rocky incline. The motor and transom were ripped right off the boat.

I got away from the water, climbing as high and as fast as I could. The waves splashed over the rocks below me. The killer whales circled around the rock a couple of times, then went back to tearing up elephant seals. A larger boat from the ship came to pick me up and gather the boat I wrecked.

It was an annual elephant seal feast for killer whales. There were hundreds of seals, young and old. The strongest and luckiest seals got away, while the weakest did not. 🐋

Farewell Gift

Roger O'Brien has been a police officer for the City of Portland since 1976. He is currently a Sergeant in the Identification Division. Roger has four children and is happily married to his second wife, Elli, who shares his love for the ocean and marine mammals.

I married my first wife Sharon in 1977. We spent our honeymoon in Vancouver, British Columbia. While at the Stanley Park Aquarium, we learned about each other's interest in cetaceans and the ocean.

Sharon and I both loved dolphins, porpoises and whales. We read stories about them and saw them whenever we could. In the late seventies we took the children to Sea World in San Diego to watch the orca shows. In the early nineties we took them to Sea World in Orlando.

As our family grew we would vacation at the Oregon Coast. Depoe Bay seemed to have many gray whales living nearby year round. The folks in the whale watching business were able to locate them whether it was during the whales' migration or not. Sharon and our children always wanted to go out whale watching, so every year we would. This was an important activity that my wife always enjoyed.

For close to fifteen years we went to the coast on the first week of August. It was the highlight of our vacation for Sharon to go out and see the gray whales. Our children and I enjoyed it, but there was some deep connection between my wife and the whales.

Sadly, like many other people, Sharon was stricken with cancer. Shortly before she died in 1994, we went on our vacation to the coast. Up to that year she had gone out to see the whales every vacation. We probably saw the same whales year after year. Often we would get within a hundred feet or closer to them. The boat would drift and the whales would swim right up to us.

Sharon was very weak from chemotherapy by this time. We rented an upper level ocean front duplex in Lincoln City. I carried her upstairs and she stayed at the apartment the whole week. There was a nice picture window and a deck where she could sit and see the ocean, but she did not go whale watching. She told me that she missed going out to see the whales, but was not strong enough to spend hours in a bouncing boat on the ocean.

One afternoon, we looked out the window towards the ocean and saw that the whales had come up to Lincoln City. We had never seen them there before. The beach there is long and shallow - the breakers start several hundred yards out from the shore. Just beyond the breakers we saw three gray whales.

We moved a chair out on the deck and Sharon, our daughter and I sat there for at least half an hour and watched the whales - it was so unexpected, and so appreciated. Then the whales disappeared.

Sharon died three weeks later. Those gray whales gave her a nice farewell gift.

Memorial

__Ralph Munro__ has been the Secretary of State of Washington since 1980. He has frequently been honored for his service to the public in areas such as voter participation, historic preservation, volunteerism, helping the developmentally disabled, and protecting the environment.

When Ralph was an Assistant to the Governor in 1975, he witnessed a gruesome capture of orca whales. This stimulated him and others to bring a successful lawsuit against Sea World, and no further whale captures have taken place in Washington State waters.

Since then, Ralph has had what he feels is an intimate relationship with orca whales in Puget Sound. He has had also a running battle with people who want to take those whales out of their natural environment, and who want to harm them.

Following the 1975 - '76 capture attempts and lawsuits, one of the whales, J 6, was named Ralph *in his honor of Ralph Munro. Ralph the whale was nicknamed* The Baby Sitter *because, although newborn orcas almost always travel right on their mother's hip,* Ralph *was often seen with baby orcas.*

Over the years I have tried to take my staff out whale watching at least once a year. On one such occasion off the west side of San Juan Island, J 6, *Ralph,* swam by and looked me in the eyes. I returned the look. I don't know what happened, but it seemed to me there was a relationship between us, something that was special and different - God granted, maybe. And this connection was something I really believed in.

When this animal disappeared in the spring of 1999 - and we knew that he had passed on - we decided to have a memorial. This came out of our desire to say good-bye to a friend, and also to continue to attract attention to the man-made difficulties whales are having. These problems are often hidden because they are underwater. We invited our friends and the press to the ceremony.

The Center for Whale Research told us they had not seen any of the local whale pods for three days. The whales had been sighted in more northern waters. My wife, Karen, was afraid we would not see whales while we were there. I kept telling her and others for two days that they would be there by 1:30, but I was just kidding everyone to keep them from being too sad. Then, Ken Balcomb called from the Center and told me the whales might actually be there around 1:30. Ken and I laughed about it, but I didn't tell Karen. She continued to say that it was a shame the whales wouldn't be around.

At exactly 1:30 P.M., the whales appeared off Lime Kiln Point where we had gathered. "There is your story right out there," I told the press. Whales were breaching, spyhopping, and tail lobbing. It was as if they came to put on a spectacular show, as if they were thanking us. What was truly special about it was the whales were led towards the shore by J 8, *Spieden - Ralph's* sister! And only whales in J pod were active.

There were people in the crowd who were absolute disbelievers in the magic of cetaceans who walked up to me afterwards and told me I was right, there was something mystical about whales. It was one of life's profound experiences.

I do not know what makes all this happen, but we had better pay attention to it. There is a problem out there in the whale's world that needs to be addressed. Scientists recently did tissue samples which showed extremely high levels of toxins in our local whales. I am convinced it is caused by the decline of the salmon stocks. The whales must eat more bottom fish which have higher toxic loads. This is part of the general decline in the Pacific Northwest environment.

This is one of the reasons we want research done with *Lolita*, a captive whale in Florida. She is an animal who was removed from the northwest in 1970. A comparative study of toxins in her system would be important for science, and for our knowledge of the whales that are here now.

What began as a simple good-bye memorial for a marine mammal friend turned into a mystical experience for many people, and seen by thousands more on television. I like to believe that events such as this give us hope.

Rescues

Noose

Mike Durban and his wife Judy have been operating the Blue Fjord *since 1987, taking folks our whale watching and observing nature in the north Vancouver Island area of British Columbia. Mike spent three years in the Galapagos Islands doing similar work. He also ran a Fisheries Patrol boat off the west coast of Vancouver Island for five years.*

In September 1984 in Johnstone Strait, a humpback whale was sighted coming through Queen Charlotte Strait into Blackfish Sound. This was unusual, as we normally see orcas and occasionally a gray whale. What made it unique was that this unfortunate whale had swum into a loop of rope, which encircled her pectoral fins. I ended up being lucky enough to get into the water with her, and cut the rope.

I had just dropped a charter group off that morning and was on my way to Telegraph Cove to pick up my wife, then head home, 200 miles south. It was the end of our season. A call came over the radio for us to keep our eyes open for a humpback. It was pea soup fog at the time, so I thought I would have to run into the whale to actually see her.

Then the whale was spotted by the folks aboard Lukwa, who discovered the humpback had a line wrapped around her. She was about thirty-five feet long, not full grown. The whale surfaced and spent about ten minutes under their bow, but it was too far out of the water and too high off the surface for someone to get close enough to her with a knife.

Most of the group of whale watching boat operators and whale researchers were nearby. There was a lot of conversation on the radio about what to do to help the whale.

The *Lukwa* stayed with the humpback for a few hours until they had to go back in. Another boat called *Gikumi* brought a flensing knife, which you don't like to mention in the same sentence as whales. They tried to tie it on a pike pole and cut the whale free, but it didn't work.

I came through a narrow pass as his whole scene was coming down the same pass towards me. I tied my boat to a mooring buoy, put on skin diving gear and got aboard the *Spy Hopper*, which was full of Japanese and German tourists whale watching.

The disabled whale was not following the usual humpback breathing mode of several short dives followed by a long dive lasting several

Humpback trapped by rope   *Photo: unknown*

minutes. Because of the line around her, the whale was not able to take deep breaths. She was making short term dives - not very far under the surface, but deep enough so that you couldn't see her.

The whale's mobility was fairly restricted. Humpback whales use their large pectoral fins for direction changes. The rope was right behind her shoulder joint, so she was not able to move those fins out. She was basically keeping mobile in order to breathe. As she had lost weight from not feeding, the noose was sliding farther down her body. There were scars marking where the rope had previously been.

Because of the whale's erratic surfacing, we could not tell where she would come up next - until a group of Pacific white-sided dolphins swam up to her. They started 'buzzbombing' the whale when she surfaced. We got right in front of the dolphins and I jumped in the water, turned around, and there was the young humpback gliding slowly towards me!

I could see the whale's eye looking at me. I stretched my arms out, knife in one hand, the other trying to grab the rope as she went by. I missed the rope by about two feet, but managed to hold my hand on the whole length of her back as she went past.

I couldn't keep up, even though she was only doing about three knots. Her momentum kept her going. I got back into the skiff. My wet suit was covered with whale lice, which interested everybody in the boat. They picked the silver dollar-sized crab-like animals off me.

We waited until the dolphins came up again, then zoomed to that spot. I jumped into the water and was directly in the path of the whale. I was vertical in the water with my hands outstretched again, right in front of her. I wondered if she would hit me.

The whale swam about five feet away as she passed by. I could see her eye scanning me once more, looking up and down with her large eye. The mouth and eye had just passed when the whale rolled her back towards me. I did not even have to swim to get hold of the rope encircling her. The rope almost came into my left hand. I grabbed onto the noose near the center of her back and, on her way down in a dive, she straightened up again still moving very slowly. I was three inches away from the back of the whale - she was all I could see.

The humpback went down about ten feet. I enjoyed this ride for a short time until I saw the knife in my right hand and remembered I was on a mission. I slipped the knife underneath the rope and took six strokes. I was holding my breath, hanging on with my left hand while cutting with my right. When the rope separated, one end fell off and came around the whale. Immediately, her fin stretched out. She began to move her other fin when it was freed. I watched as her shoulders began to move and sensed the relief she felt at being able to move again. The whale swam on, and I floated to the surface.

Everyone was ecstatic that we were successful, and we had a great celebration that evening.

The rope was a noose that the whale probably swam into because it was floating on the surface. Other scars suggest there were other lines or net connected with the nylon line I cut. The rope might have been in a kelp mat. Humpbacks like to play in that stuff. They stick their faces into the kelp and scratch around. There was a lot of discussion about it with whale scientists, but it was all speculation.

A buddy of mine mentioned this event to a local newspaper. My uncle runs a lodge in the area, and he had somebody from CBC staying there. A couple of days later it was all over the country in the news. My mother said, "It's nice to hear something good for a change!"

Ten days later, the whale was sighted one hundred miles south - so, most likely, she will be okay.

Beached

Roberto Bubas is a Park Ranger at the Peninsula Valdes National Park in Argentina. Roberto's story No Fear *is on page 6.*

In July 1995, during our winter, a right whale and her calf were inside the inlet where I live on the Peninsula Valdes. Sometimes, when the current is very strong, shallow banks of pebbles are created in the mouth of the inlet. It is very dangerous for the whales when the tide drops. The current goes very fast over these shallows, and it can take the whales and put them on the banks of pebbles. This is what happened - the right whale mother got stranded at sunset.

I saw the beached whale and went to her in my kayak. The sea was very choppy and dangerous because of the strong current. It was four in the afternoon, low tide was at six. The high tide would be six hours later. I felt there was very little probability that the whale would survive because there was so long a time between low and high tide.

When I first got to the whale I chased away the sea gulls. There were many birds which had heard the cries of the whale. It was a very sad, moaning sound. I began to make a hole under the whale's pectoral fins with my paddle so her lungs would not become too compressed. I threw water on the whale's back for four hours.

It became dark and windy. I called on the radio, and a lot of people came to help. We had to wait some distance away from the whale by a small shelter. There was nothing else to do. By eleven o'clock, we could no longer hear the blows of the whale. We thought she had died. I called on the radio to the ships offshore. With their radar, they looked for the whale. They found her four kilometers away, swimming in the sea!

The next day we went on motorcycles along the beach forty kilometers south and forty kilometers north, and we searched with a small airplane, but we saw no dead whales. She was alive! She must have gotten herself off at high tide in the dark. Two months later, whale watchers using photo identification of scars and white marks on the mother whale's back found her alive with her calf.

In Our Net

Dan Dole has been a commercial fisherman in Alaska for ten of the past twenty years. He fell in love with both the beauty of southeast Alaska, and the challenge of working on the water with the tides and currents while making the net the most effective tool possible. He teaches high school French and Latin in the Northwest.

We were purse seining off Little Roller Bay, on the west side of Noyes Island in southeast Alaska. I was the 'jump-off man' in the skiff. John Lunde was the 'skiff man.' John would drive the skiff, towing the seine net as close to the shore as the tides, currents and ocean bottom would allow. The other end of the net went back through the water to the much larger seine boat, the *Shannon*, in a long J-shaped arc. Always moving up or down the beach with the current, skipper Pat would decide when the net had been out long enough and was most likely full of salmon. He would bring the *Shannon* around towards the skiff, almost making a circle out of the net.

John and I would then bring the shore end of the net back to the boat, where the rest of the crew would use the deck winch to close the purse (bottom) of the net with the purse line. The power block on the boom would be used to pull in the rest of the net. Whatever fish had swum into the net would be hoisted up and over the rail onto the deck.

I did not even notice it happening, but all of a sudden there was a big commotion in the net about thirty yards behind the skiff on the beach end. John and I looked and saw a whale. We saw it spout once. It had obviously hit the net and was not happy about the whole thing.

Pat talked with John over the radio. We first drove the skiff back down the beach, trying to pull the net away from and off the whale. But the whale was stuck, so we cast off the skiff from the net. John took me back and I got onto the *Shannon* and joined the crew hauling the net back aboard. We were all watching to see if the whale was still caught as the net was hauled in. We did not see the whale for a long time, so we kept 'hauling gear'.

When the part of the net where the whale was started coming to the surface, maybe one hundred feet off our stern, we saw that our net was obviously distressed by the weight of the whale. We were using the power block to pull in the net with this very large animal in it. It was

Humpback in purse seine net   *Photo: Dan Dole*

much more weight than a large load of fish. When the whale got closer
to the boat, it started flailing around. We could see the net over the
back of the whale, stuck on all the bumps around its head, nose and
front flippers. We could watch the mesh splitting on the whale's back
as it struggled.

It was a humpback whale, probably forty feet long. It had swum
under the cork line, which holds the top edge of the net at the surface of
the water, and was surfacing with the net over its nose. The whale
eventually broke through the net and swam out safely. It might have
been twenty minutes before the whale broke free. I don't think it was
hurt at all by the encounter.

We hauled the rest of the net on board and headed for Steamboat
Bay, about an hour's run from our location. When we got there, we
piled the net on the dock and proceeded to spend a good day and a half
putting it back together.

We stitched a big 'starfish' of new web into the huge hole the whale
made so we could go back out and try to fish some more that day.
Eventually we cut that entire section out and replaced it with a clean
strip of web.

Whales usually sense the presence of the net so well even the young ones rarely get caught up in it. It would be interesting to see, through an underwater camera, what happens when they swim up to a net, put the brakes on, and change course. ➤

Go That Way

Scott Fratcher and his wife Allison live aboard and travel on their sailboat. Scott's story Oops! *is on page 56.*

We were in San Carlos, Mexico, on the mainland side of the Sea of Cortez, when we got a call that some people were coming to charter our boat out of La Paz. We ran straight to La Paz in roughly three days. We have a forty-two foot sailboat, a steel hulled, Colvin-designed *Saugeen Witch*.

About four hundred miles from La Paz, we started to observe more sea life than we had ever seen. We were in a massive school of dolphins. A huge pod started surfacing underneath the bowsprit. We reached down and briefly touched their backs.

We got to La Paz, picked our guests up, turned around and went back out for a ten day trip. They were very interested in dolphins and whales, but we did not see anything in the way of marine mammals for nine days. After day five, we had people looking out on both sides of the boat all the time trying to find any type of sea life that we could show them, but there was none. This was very unusual, especially since we had seen so much just before this trip.

On the last day when we were in the channel on our way back into La Paz, we saw a bunch of activity. Sixteen sperm whales had beached themselves the night before. They had been on the beach for a tide cycle-and-a-half. The Mexican Navy had military teams around, but they were not doing anything to get the stranded whales off.

There were five whales on the beach to the left. On the right were the other eleven. As the tide began rising, the whales were attempting to push themselves farther up the beach, and people were trying different things to help the stranded whales.

One group was trying to tie seatbelt-like nylon webbing around the whales' tails and attempting to pull them backwards. It was not working. It was cutting big grooves into the whales' skin.

Other people tried taking a big, fast dinghy into the shallow water right in front of the whale. As the whale was attempting to move farther into the shallow water, he would be forced to stop or swim into the loud dinghy.

We anchored our sailboat and found an unattended whale. We observed that the method which worked best was having eight or nine people get into the water with the whale, so positioned ourselves between the whale and the beach. People put their hands onto the whale and pushed, keeping steady pressure as they were kicking, trying to get the whale into deeper water. As the tide and a slight swell came in, we felt the whale float. When we were all pushing, he would back up just a bit.

The whale we were working on was lying on the beach at about a forty-five degree angle. The farthest forward people were just ahead of his eye. Then seven or eight other people were in a line aft along the whale's side. We were pushing on the whale's left, forward side. When the swell came in, the whale would back off, moving to his right which would push him into deeper water. As soon as the pressure was gone from people pushing on him, he would give a little kick with his fluke and slide himself back up on the beach again.

As soon as the whale started to pull off, whoever was pushing closest to the whale's head would release his pressure and move in front of the whale - placing his body between the beach and the whale's huge square head - then the animal would stop. He would not swim past us.

There was one point when I was pushing right by the whale's eye. I was looking into his eye. It had a look of deep sadness. What tragedy had occurred in that pod's life to cause this self-destructive act?

The whale continued trying to get farther up onto the beach. No matter how much it seemed the whale wanted to be up on the beach, he just would not push past you, although he could have easily done it. There was nothing that kept the whale from giving one kick with his fluke and ignoring all of us. Even if he did not land on us or physically hurt us, he could have simply moved us out of his way.

We kept working together, pushing him off bit by bit. As the tide came in, we got the whale into deeper water until he was floating. As soon as he was in the channel he started swimming very slowly, making a big loop.

We were trying to get him back out the channel to the sea. Because

Sperm whale being guided after rescue   Photo: Scott Fratcher

of the way the whale was pointing when he came off the beach, we had to make him turn in a two hundred degree arc to face out to sea. People kept swimming next to the whale while he made his turn. As long as people were next to him on each side, the whale kept going nice and slowly down the channel. It was easy to swim fast enough to keep up with him.

Every now and then, he would make a ninety degree turn and start heading right for the beach. When someone got in front of him he would stop. I think he went back up on the beach two more times before he ended up leaving the channel. The second time he beached himself I got our dinghy so I could pace him on one side. People were in the water swimming on either side of the whale. It was a mad house. The whale started to make a turn for the beach again. I accelerated hard in the dinghy to get right in front of him. The top of his head was three feet under the water. He was clearly heading for the beach.

I tried to get on an intercept course with him. As I got to where I figured that would be, the engine stalled. Just as it died, the whale came up to breathe. I was directly in his path. When he got six feet away from me, he started slowing down dramatically.

When his head was a foot and a half from the dinghy, the whale came to a complete stop. He stayed there for six or seven seconds motionless on the surface. It seemed to me like this animal was making a decision. The whale then turned away from me and my ten foot dinghy and started swimming down the channel towards the sea again. I started the motor and returned to pacing him.

The channel was almost a mile long and my wife was getting tired keeping up with the whale all that way. About a half mile from the channel's mouth, she swam over to the whale and grabbed onto his dorsal fin. The whale was swimming on the surface and did not seem to mind. Every time the whale tried to swim to the left, my wife would quickly push off and get between the whale and the beach.

We paced him right out to the end of the channel. When we arrived at the edge of the sea, he came to a complete stop, waited about ten seconds, and then slowly rolled over spilling my wife off his dorsal fin and clearing himself from the people around him. He then slowly accelerated about fifty feet from us. Once completely clear, he put on a great burst of speed and dove. We never saw him again.

I felt the whale knew we were attempting to help him, and that slow roll at the mouth of the channel ended any doubt I had that the whale was a highly intelligent, gentle animal who understood what we were doing.

As the whales left and swam down the coast, six of them beached themselves in Belandra, the next little bay. Nobody did anything about them. After we had worked so hard to get them off the first beach, it was anticlimactic, and there was a general consensus that there was very little we could do for them. We thought was that if we forced them off of that beach, they probably would go somewhere else and just do it again. It was sad that those six whales ended up dying so soon after their rescue. ✍

It's Our Job

Sheila Dean and her husband Bob Schoelkopf are co-directors of the Marine Mammal Stranding Center in Brigantine, New Jersey.

We are part of the Northeast Stranding Network, which covers Maine to Virginia. Not every state has a coordinated stranding network or facilities for animals. Some states rely on groups from other areas to rescue and care for animals from their beaches. For instance,

Delaware has people who will go and pick animals up, but they do not have any place to put them. They send stranded cetaceans to us or to the National Aquarium in Baltimore. Our facility is very small, so we are limited as to what we can do and how many animals we can care for. Many times we have to tell people who have rescued dolphins, porpoises or seals that our pools are filled.

We have volunteers in with the cetaceans all the time to protect the animals from banging into the sides of the pool until they are accustomed to swimming in such a confined space. Our first pool was so small it was difficult for them to maneuver.

Since we started the Stranding Center in 1977, we have handled quite a few types of whales including minke, True's beaked, goose beaked, Antillean beaked, pilot, grampus, humpbacks, fin and sperm whales.

Some of the experiences were more sad than happy. By the time we get a call about a whale stranding, there is danger of the animal dying either from ailment or human-related causes such as propellor hits or ingestion of plastics. Propellor hits are a common cause of death to the greater whales on the New Jersey coast, like the fin and humpbacks, because a lot of large ships travel along the East Coast.

We have had young seventeen foot sperm whales that were hit by boats. We assume the mother was killed because the animals were very emaciated and wandering by themselves. Pneumonia often sets in which can kill the whale.

We were called by the federal government to respond to a stranded thirty foot humpback whale at Ocean City, Maryland seven years ago. It was a cold winter day. Apparently, two days earlier, federal and state officials had tried unsuccessfully to tow the whale off the sandbar by his tail. We've known for many years that this is probably the worst way to attempt to remove an animal; not only can you separate the vertebrae, you can also cause the animal to panic with the fear of drowning, from being towed backwards. We have developed a padded line which is draped around the animal allowing us to pull it in a forward facing position.

Once it is off the sandbar, the animal is able to continue swimming and diving, but it cannot swim to either side. As long as the power of the boat is moving the whale forward it has to follow the boat, but it is still able to come up and take a breath and dive. We have been successful in moving large whales with this harness, as well as smaller ani-

Volunteer Michelle Garrity walking a common dolphin, which was later released - a rehabilitation first.

Photo: Bob Schoelkopf, MMSC

mals with a small version of the harness.

The thirty foot humpback had to lift his pectoral fin up over my head while I put the line under it. The whale knew it was being assisted. It could have killed me just by dropping his fin. I had no fear of that.

We dealt with a dead right whale that was in the surf, whose tail was lobbed off by a freighter. Ironically the same whale, two months prior to being killed, was in our inlet with an adult female. We photographed him at that time. The whale had apparently gone through the shipping lane where his tail was lobbed off, and he washed ashore in a State Park.

We tried to secure the whale in the surf. I was alongside him putting a cable around the pectoral fin to pull him further up on shore. A wave came and picked the animal up, causing a suction that drew me under it. When the wave receded, I was stuck under the whale. I held my breath, waiting for the next wave to come in so I could get out. The people on the beach were not sure what was going on. They could not pull me out with the safety line because of the weight of the whale. Fortunately, the dead animal did lift up with the next large wave.

While we attempted in heavy surf to secure the dead animal, the female we photographed him with was off the coast showing behavior neither I nor other researchers had seen before with right whales. She would lift her pectoral fin out of the water and wave it back and forth. She stayed there for two days off the coast. This same female was sighted for seven years after that. We have seen her with two calves and have videos of her nursing one of the calves all day long.

My wife and I began as dolphin trainers. We did dolphin shows and Sheila performed underwater ballet with a thousand pound sea lion. The animal was raised from a yearling. After about seven years we felt depleted and useless to the animals. We could not do much other than feed them. And, we felt very badly about them being in captivity.

Because we had done dolphin shows, we received a call in 1976 about a pygmy sperm whale stranded on the beach in Atlantic City. We found a twelve foot long male, still alive. The City Public Works was about to put a line on his tail and try to pick him up with a front end loader, carry him out to the surf and lay him in the water. We immediately stopped them. I ended up spending two hours in the surf in forty-two degree water and street clothes trying to get the animal refloated. We took an inflatable raft from the Coast Guard (deflated at the time), rolled the animal in it, then inflated the raft and towed it about four miles to the Coast Guard base.

We sat in wet suits with the whale round the clock . After five days of feeding him through a tube and giving him medication, the whale died. We were pretty depressed. We did the necropsy and found that the animal had died of old age. It was ironic because while we were trying to pump him full of steroids to revive him, the whale just wanted to die in peace.

This was the first wild animal we worked on. We realized there was a lot more to marine mammals than performing. They need help in the wild where they face propellor injuries and pollution from heavy metals, chemicals, and plastics that are either deliberately or inadvertently dumped by boats or which wash in from shore.

There is nothing like a whale in the wild. You never see the same

Volunteers and lifeguards assist MMSC staff
in the recovery of an injured Risso's dolphin,
Brigantine, New Jersey

Photo: MMSC

spirit in the eye of a captive animal as you see in one in the wild.

When a cetacean comes in and has to be put in an indoor pool, volunteers are with the animal twenty-four hours a day. These 'whale walkers' are set up on an hour and a half shift interval. They are in the water simply holding the animal. We do not allow any stroking, although some vocalization is allowed because the animals seem to respond to that to a degree.

Here is an animal that has never been on land in her life, and has never had any association with a human. We are aliens to the whale. But there are two things we have in common with whales which they share with their family in the ocean. One is our heartbeat; the other is the warmth of our body. The animal responds to these and immediately realizes we are there to help, not hurt them. They may also be able to read our minds, but that is a difficult concept to verify.

As the animal starts to recuperate, there are certain people that it likes and certain people that it doesn't. We had a common dolphin who would snap at one gentleman every time he got into the pool, but would not snap at anyone else.

We were caring for a pilot whale. When I went to feed it for the first time, it swallowed not only the fish but also my hand up to the elbow. Their teeth are fairly sharp, and there is a lot of power. I winced from the pain but did not attempt to pull my hand out. When I tightened my muscles, the animal immediately opened his mouth and let me remove my hand. I got another fish and offered it again. This time the whale simply grabbed very lightly, got the fish and sucked it gently into his mouth.

The pilot whale enjoyed taking my hand in his mouth. I would rub his tongue and tickle it, and he would pull me around the pool with my hand in his mouth. This animal was eventually transferred to an aquarium for long term care. Sometimes I would visit him. When I approached the aquarium - even before I entered the building - the whale started behaving as though he realized I was there. He was too aggressive for the trainers and handlers at the facility to get in the pool with him. The whale would smack at them with his tail and bite at them. But when I got in the pool he would immediately take my hand in his mouth and pull me around. We would play for a couple of hours. He would toss me in the air and swim around with me. He was a really great animal. Unfortunately, a yeast infection settled in his stomach and he bled to death one night.

When an animal strands, it is most often due to a bad injury or a serious illness. Given a well-equipped facility, it will take a while for the animal to get better and then strengthened enough to survive in the wild again. If rehab people say they have him for one day, and then let him loose, they did nothing for the animal. It takes time. We can learn a lot about an animal's condition from tests and blood samples.

Unfortunately, no one has a facility big enough for the large whales. Simply moving an animal the size of a fin or minke whale is very hard on it. They are so delicate, you need to have just the right equipment and knowledge.

Fitting a stranded young humpback whale with a forward-tow harness to move it into deeper water. Ocean City, Maryland

Dedicating our lives to helping marine mammals has been an interesting combination of rewarding and disappointing experiences. There is not a high success rate with stranded cetaceans. We wish we could do more for them, but we just do not know enough about them. Few veterinarians, or vet school students, actually study whales, dolphins and porpoises.

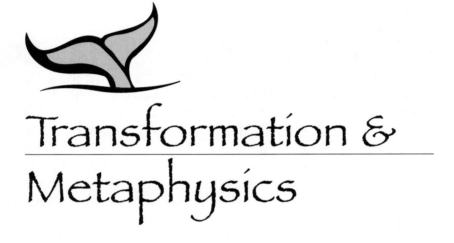

Transformation & Metaphysics

I Was a Whale

Kim Gannaway grew up in Minnesota and is an Intensive Care Unit Nurse, with a deep love for whales.

I knew whales were out there in the ocean, somewhere. But here in Minnesota there was nothing to make me have any connection with them. I was into dogs and horses.

In 1990, a man I had been dating went berserk. He tried to kill me. I could not believe I was being attacked by someone I knew, that it was not a horrible dream or an hallucination. He was strangling me, and as I was losing consciousness from not being able to breathe, I quit struggling for air. I did not feel the need to breathe any more. I just got very tired. I thought this was how I was going to die, and I thought how sad my mom was going to be that this happened. I was worried about her.

Then everything in my mind went dark and gray. Over and over I had the vision of gray and blue, the feeling of rolling and freedom. I could not see where I was going, in the gray-blue. I was going forward, peacefully and freely. I was not worried about bumping into anything. I knew where I was going. Before this man could murder me, my roommate and her boyfriend came home and heard the noises from my room. They kicked the door down, got him off me, and took me to the hospital. My attacker went to jail.

While I was recovering, the vision kept coming back to me: the gray, the blue, the rolling, the freedom. What was that? I was bothered because everybody else was talking about seeing a 'white light' in near-death experiences. If I was dying, why didn't I see the 'white light'? This added to my discomfort. Not only was I battered and bruised, physically and emotionally, but the spiritual aspect of my life was out of sync.

I spent a great deal of time recuperating in bed, much of it thinking about my vision. The more I thought about it the less it made sense. Finally it came to me. I told my mom, "I was a whale!" She told me to get more rest. She thought I was nuts. Whenever I would tell people this explanation of my vision, I was met with a similar reaction. Nobody would take me seriously.

I began to watch television programs about whales. I did not connect with it fully until I saw a special program about Christopher Reeve.

Whales were coming up all around his boat. When I saw the whales going through the water, rolling through the gray-blue liquid, I realized that is exactly what I saw. Then I saw Christopher Reeve touch a whale. He was talking about how moving and powerful an experience it was. I knew I had go and find out for myself.

I read a book called *The Friendly Whales* and called the whale watching company they recommended in San Diego. I told the woman about my experience and she encouraged me to come. Unlike everyone else I talked to, this woman understood the connection between whales and humans. In 1996, I flew to San Diego and went on a whale watching trip. No one I knew at home would go with me. It made no sense to them, but it was something I knew in my heart I needed to do. At that time, my life was like Hell. I couldn't get over the experience of what had happened. I focused on it. Everybody said I needed to get over it - but how could I? I had no idea what I was in for when I got on board the boat but, in a way, I knew this was an important gift I was giving to myself.

On the first two days, we saw whales. They came close, but no touching. The whale calves were very young. Their mothers would parade them by the boat and seemed to show them off. We were out in smaller boats, pangas, with Mexican captains taking us around the lagoon to see the whales. On our last day, I was getting desperate. It was cold and very choppy on the water. No one had touched a whale. We had only three hours left. I needed to make this connection. And yet the whales would come within inches and tease me, staying just out of my reach. As the sun began to set, I had resigned myself to the fact that this was not going to happen.

The young whales would pump their tail fluke and slide up and over their mama's head back into the water. All of a sudden, a huge mother whale and her young baby came alongside the boat very slowly. They were about ten feet away. The mom would come to the surface, take a big breath of air and just hang there for a bit. I yelled, "Oh my God - our boat is really small!" The whale and her baby started coming closer. When the baby came up, I yelled, "Look how cute he is!" Then it seemed as if they went away. All of a sudden, there was a spyhop right off the front of the panga. Big head, with the eye looking at us. As they circled the panga, it felt like they were taunting me. The mother went under us, inches away. Her head was starting to come out and she still had thirty feet of body to go.

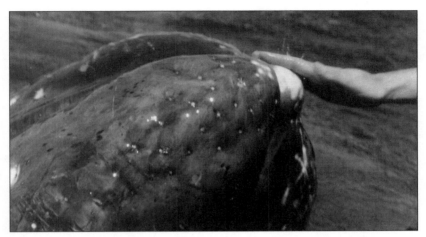

Healing touch with gray whale   Photo: Kim Gannaway

I lost my mind. I went into the water. I stuck my arms way in, up to my face. I could feel the electricity - she was millimeters away - but I could not touch her. Somebody had to grab me - one of the guys in the boat had me by the back of the pants.

I got really sad because I did not get to touch her. I thought she was dancing for me because I was in the front of the panga, and that's where she was. I did not want anybody to see me cry, so I hung over the bow of the boat, with my hands in the water, thinking, "I need to touch you. I need to know that you are real to me." This overwhelming sadness came over me. I thought I would not make the connection between why this happened to me and the vision which I experienced as I was nearly dying.

And then, the baby whale was under me. It was as if the mama felt my need and let her baby come for me. I reached out and he let my fingers slide along his full length from head to tail as he swam past. The smoothness, the coolness, and the little bumps were electric.

Then they were gone. The baby and his mother gave me that gift, as if they knew what I needed. I started screaming and crying. It impressed me deeply that the mother allowed her calf to do that for me. I made the connection. I had to grab my head, which felt like it was spinning around. It was quite a release of powerful emotions. I felt embarrassed as the people in the panga witnessed me losing it. I had not shared my past, or my vision, with these people. When I touched

Kim Gannaway after touching gray whale   Photo: Paul Glasper

the young whale I felt the gray, the blue, the cold and the rolling. The baby whale rolled right under my hand and finger tips, cold and smooth and free. I connected, and that's why I couldn't stop crying. I had completed my mission. I was so happy I was not nuts. This is what I had seen as I was near-death. I cried for myself, for the pain that I had gone through. At that point I said good-bye to all the pain that man had caused me. I was done, and I feel that this whale let me live again.

Back in Minnesota I was not afraid anymore. I didn't dwell on that man; he was dead to me. He, and fear, were not going to run my life anymore. I remember forever my baby whale: cold, gray and free. I know everything in my world is okay.

Be Here Now

Dan Harpole has been a resident of Port Townsend since 1981. Dan's story Put In Our Place *is on page 18.*

I grew up in Portland and had not been around the water much. In March 1980, I was going into my last quarter of college. It had been a long, trying time. Evergreen was my fourth college, and I was finally going to graduate, much to my parent's delight, and my own as well. I received an internship at The Whale Museum in Friday Harbor to help create a video on whales of Puget Sound.

It was mid-March, and the San Juan Islands, as much as they can be beautiful and glorious, can also be incredibly dreary, isolating and lonely. The latter is what I was experiencing. I had developed a number of friendships at Evergreen, which I was missing. I was living in the loft of a tiny cabin and not all happy, wondering what I was doing in such an remote spot.

Although this whole 'whale thing' seemed like a groovy notion in a lot of ways, I was asking myself what the big deal really was. They are just some big animals that are out there living in the water. I was walking along South Beach commiserating with myself. It was one of those dreary gray Northwest days where you cannot tell where the sky stops and the sea starts, in a way that gets people depressed. I was wondering again what I was doing there, when suddenly there was a commotion in the water.

A pod of whales was coming south in San Juan Channel. Another was coming down Haro Strait. They met up and started frolicking twenty feet offshore. The whole sea was in turmoil. Whales splashed, breached, tail lobbed, pectoral fin slapped, spyhopped; what many people term 'play.'

This experience permanently altered the way I viewed this inland sea. While moments earlier this was a bleak, somber, and foreboding environment, now it was full of joy and wonder because whales were jumping around in front of me. It seemed like they were having a great time, and I recognized that I ought to be enjoying myself, too.

I Love Big Women!

Sheri Bell *worked with the ELSA Wild Animal Appeal, an international organization helping animals around the world. She taught in schools about endangered, threatened and extinct animals. Sheri was with the Mountain Lion Foundation in Sacramento for five years working to stop the sport hunting of mountain lions. She now works as a docent for stranded sea lions at the Marine Mammal Center of Sausalito, on Pier 39 in San Francisco. Sheri is also a legislative advocate at the Capitol in Sacramento.*

On Easter morning, we were four hours out of Dana Point, California, on our way to the gray whale breeding lagoons on the Baja Peninsula. A pod of orcas came up and did some 'entertaining' beside our boat. They flew through the air in formation and showed other display activities. The crew on the boat had never seen orcas there and quit whatever tasks they were doing to watch. We all ran to the side the orcas were on. The boat tipped as everybody took pictures.

We got to the lagoon and saw a lot of gray whales. They were feeding, playing, giving birth, and mating. The little ones were learning to breach and doing all kinds of humorous things.

Then we went out in the lagoon, aboard fifteen foot skiffs, six of us at a time. The first time out, a baby surfaced right beside us. His forty-five foot long mother also came up beside us. My husband was astounded. There was never any feeling of fear or intimidation. The mother laid right under the skiff where we could have touched her. We pet the baby and the mother lay there and watched our every move.

The guide said sometimes a baby would get hurt by the boat, maybe by rubbing against the engine, and the mother wouldn't bat an eye. She seemed to know it was not intentional. But, he said, if you lifted a hand to her baby she would turn the boat over. Of course, no one had any intention of doing that.

One of the men on the trip was Leo, an Assistant District Attorney from Los Angeles. On the trip south, he was very cynical about seeing the whales. He said he had only come along to learn how to bring his own boat to the lagoon. Out in the skiff, however, he was affected by the presence of the whales. Instead of the babies, who everybody else petted, he fell in love with the mothers. He would lean out of the skiff and yell at the top of his lungs, "I love big women!" These forty ton whales would come over to the boat when he yelled. One female whale in particular would not let us go back to the big boat if this man was with us in the skiff. She would get between us and the big boat and keep us away from it as long as she wanted to be around Leo. The guys running the trip said they had never seen a mother whale be that interested in someone. It was wonderful to see him interacting; and, he was no longer cynical.

One day we went out and there were no whales. My husband started singing at the top of his lungs, "Momma, Don't Let Your Babies Grow Up to be Cowboys." All of a sudden the water was alive. The whales came at us; it was almost scary because they seemed so interested in the song, or the vibes, or whatever.

In Africa we saw lions up close, one charged our van because we surprised him. There is an element of terror around lions which I have never felt around whales. I've done animal welfare work for thirty years and after thinking about it a lot, I've concluded there is simply a feeling of peacefulness surrounding cetaceans. I am aware of tremendous love and interspecies connection which I don't feel with big cats. While they are impressive to observe, if you take one step outside the van, you will be their lunch. There is the feeling that if you fell out of the boat into the water full of whales, you would not be harmed.

On the voyage back to Dana Point we were asked to critique the trip. They started with Leo. "I came down here to see how to bring my own boat. I would not know one whale from another, or care. And then...met a whale...and I thank God for it." He started to cry. Then everybody cried, because we had seen the change in him, and felt it within ourselves, within this week's time. It was such a spiritually wonderful experience, we were all changed.

Beloved Whales

Rita Comp has been teaching in Southern California for almost forty years. She has written many short stories about children. Rita is teaching her grandchild to figure skate, and loves playing the piano.

My friend Kathy and I were very excited about going to see the gray whales. A week before we went out, we put in our request to Great

Spirit in the Whale Kingdom to have an encounter with the whales.

I said, "Beloved whales, we are going to be coming out into the ocean again. Last time one of the mothers came to the boat and showed us her calf, which was a very spiritual experience for me. So, if you, dear whales, would just let us meet with you again, we would be so grateful." Having sent out a little prayer to the whales, Kathy and I boarded the boat thinking, or hoping, we would really see a whale.

The ocean was rough. We were having ten foot swells which threw salt water into our faces. I shouted, "Just one breach, that's all I'm asking." It took about thirty seconds. A whale appeared about a hundred-and-fifty feet off the boat and breached. A woman standing next to me asked how this worked. I told her that projecting vibrations of love and calmness were most effective.

I demonstrated with a little song: "Beautiful, beautiful whales; I'll love you forever more." I urged the other people to just sing a song of appreciation and thanks. "Just make up anything that lets you project calm, loving vibrations." They said, "You lead us in a song!" I said, "No, No. You each need to do it quietly in your own mind. When we are all doing it together we are not as calmly focused. Each of you do it." Almost instantly, a beautiful gray whale appeared alongside the boat, about a hundred feet off, and breached. The captain announced the whales were in a playful mood, and they had only seen four breaches so far this season.

We experienced reassuring vibrations and playful antics from the whales for our three and a half hour trip. When the captain said she needed to turn back because we were running out of gas, Kathy said, "Well, let's ask for a grand finale!"

I said, "Oh no. You know, anything more they give us is from their generosity. I can't ask them again. Think of the energy it takes for a creature the size of a school bus to hurl itself up into the air breaching."

Her wish was granted. As a final farewell a large whale cut across our bow very slowly. It accompanied us a short way. Some of us were yelling, "We love you! We thank you!" We felt they had to know how much we cared. This, to us, was clearly a validation of the oneness between all species. As I left the boat, I was astonished when people thanked me. Apparently they felt I connected them to the whales.

That night before I fell asleep, I asked to join the whales' consciousness in the sleep state. I experienced an electron wavelike cyclical-intermingling of soothing comfort and joy in my dreams.

Cosmic Requests

Leslie Stager has been an Earth guide at wilderness camps. Leslie was a very desert-oriented person, and had no connection with the ocean before her first trip to Hawaii, where she went on a whale watching trip and heard the humpback whales call her. Since 1992, Leslie has worked as a labor and delivery hospice nurse, a massage therapist and a silk painter.

In Hawaii, I spent the winter swimming regularly. Every time I dove under the water I would hear humpback whales singing. Eventually, as spring arrived, they started to leave on their migration to Alaska. There were fewer and fewer whales. I would dive under the boat and hear nothing, no sounds of the whales. I would feel disappointed, thinking whale season was finally over. Every single time I would mentally ask, "Are there any whales out there at all?", I would hear the singing of a whale. I began to feel as if they were responding to my question.

One day when I went out in a boat, I said, "All I really want is to put my head under the water and see a whale, to see what it looks like underwater." I said that request out loud to everyone on the boat. I put my head into the water and looked around. The visibility was not great. I was hanging out down there holding my breath, watching. Suddenly, I realized I was looking right at a mother and baby humpback whale, less than thirty feet away! I got so excited I began to scream underwater through my snorkel. It felt like a direct response to my request.

The first day I was out on a research boat, I thought I would like to see a mom and her baby come up to the boat. Soon after thinking those thoughts, we came upon a mom, her baby and an escort. The mom and baby started swimming over to the boat. We were all hanging over the side looking at them in awe.

I was supposed to be taking photographs. I could not do it. I was shaking with excitement, feeling their tremendous power. I felt a strong connection with the mother and calf.

I suddenly sensed a great energy behind me. I turned and saw the escort whale spyhopping next to the boat! I watched as this huge dark figure rose silently out of the water and looked at us. He then sunk into the water. The sense of silence was overwhelming. We were in a fifteen foot rigid inflatable and he loomed above the boat right over me.

None of us would have seen him if I hadn't turned, because we were so focused on the mom and her baby on the other side.

I thought that was it for the day. Then we saw activity up ahead. A group of males were in a 'heat run.' It's believed they are trying to get a particular female to mate with them. It was as if the males were at war with each other. The whales were in a long line moving at twelve knots or faster. They were swimming over, under and around each other, smashing together. They would bash into each other underwater with their chins.

Big waves were being made by tons of whales moving closely together. Sometimes they would rise out of the water. When they came down there were bellowing sounds, perhaps from the air in their lungs being pushed out of their blowhole. They were moving so quickly it was all we could do to keep up with them in our inflatable. We could never get ahead of them. They swam in a mile long circle, continuing this activity of smashing on each other for about an hour. One whale's dorsal fin was almost torn off. Another had a bloody face and chin.

At any one time there were twelve to fifteen whales on the surface, with many others underwater. More whales swam across the bay to join in the heat run. Others would back out of the group as they got tired. It was a huge humpback whale war.

At times the whales would all go underwater at once. We would not know where they were, so we just kept powering ahead. Suddenly the whales surfaced, surrounding the boat. We were in the midst of a huge energy caused by the largest creatures on Earth in their most powerful behavior. We were awed by the force around us, surrounded by aggressive male humpback whales.

They were completely aware of our boat. They never ran into us and we never ran into them, even though twenty fifty-foot long humpbacks were surfacing directly in front of us and swimming inches away as we powered along with them at top speed.

Finally, after about an hour of following them, we realized there was no way we would be able to go into the water to document them. Again, I had the thought that this was as good as it gets. We left them and I figured we'd see no more whales that day.

But I said to the cosmos anyway, if I could see anything else, I would like to witness dolphins interacting with whales.

Almost immediately, as we headed towards Molokai, we saw a baby humpback lolling about in the water. He was upside down on his back, waving his pectoral fins around in the air like a kid in a swimming pool. His mom was nearby. Five bottlenose dolphins were playing with the baby whale, leaping over his belly and swimming under and around him. The baby whale was rolling back and forth in the warm water, enjoying being the center of the dolphins attention. The dolphins came up to our boat. We got into the water and swam briefly with them. Then they went back to play with the young whale.

The experiences of the day were overwhelming. Everything which I had asked to see appeared. But the day was not over yet.

The next event was finding a 'singer,' a whale that can be heard on the surface, through the boat.

I got in the water and dove under. The sound of the humpback was so loud I could feel the sonic vibration moving through my whole body. It felt like I was surrounded by huge loudspeakers. There was only one whale singing, and there were no other boats around, so it was the only sound - one voice coming in at maximum intensity and volume.

There is something powerful in the humpback song. Although I don't know what they are saying, or what it means, it feels like being enveloped in a knowing, or awareness of something very deep, profound, and ancient.

The whales have been on the Earth for so long they carry the wisdom of ancient times. There is something very familiar in their singing. I had listened to it a lot during my daily swim, and it almost sent me into a trance state. It drew me down, deeper under the water. It was a struggle to come back up. There was an incredible hunger in me to hear what they were saying. I came out of the water and felt as if my life had changed in some significant way.

Whales are very aware of human beings and are making connections. A lot of people are becoming aware of this. I know a researcher whose spiritual awakening came through working with whales. How she viewed the world shifted from her exposure to these animals.

Their intelligence is vast and their means of communication is much grander than anything we know. The whales are affecting us on many levels. They get us out of our minds and into experiencing something beyond ourselves.

I feel the whales are somehow guiding my life. They entered into my body and spirit. I have no idea what comes next, except that I will keep following them. I am called to introduce more people to whales, in part by sharing these stories.

A Guide to Being

Terry J. Walker is the author of How To Swim With Dolphins, A Guide to Being, *and* Dolphin Healing, Dolphin Heart. *She lives in Hawaii with her fisherman husband Norman.*

When I first started swimming with dolphins, I became so fanatical I could not stand being out of the water. I had to be with them. I wondered why I was so addicted. I meditated about it, and the dolphins said: "It's your job to share the joy." I love my job.

In 1995, I quit working as a teacher to be able to swim full time with spinner dolphins. I was tired of being limited to swimming with them only on weekends. I started a research project to find out about dolphin communication. I wanted to be friends with them. I have achieved this by sending mental pictures, feelings and intentions to them, as well as having conversations with spoken words.

Communicating with cetaceans is a 'knowing' beyond words. It is a sense that conveys itself through all the ways we receive information. I have identified different ways dolphins communicate: body language, distance, depth and proximity.

Dolphins are very energetic. They are quite skilled at reading other animals' energy. In thousands of interactions, I have had only three negative experiences. After being chased out of the water by a grouchy dolphin, I began to pay attention to what dolphins do with their bodies, actions and energy when they do not want to be around people. I think we can coexist in the water if humans learn how to pay attention and respond to dolphins' signals.

I grew up in Hawaii. When I was twelve years old we went to the beach, my sister, some neighborhood kids and I waded out in the water. It was murky and you could not see the bottom. I was the furthest out, and something swam between my legs. I wasn't scared at all. I reached down and grabbed it with the first try and pulled up. It was the dorsal fin of a baby spinner dolphin. It stayed with me, and gave me a ride! It was about four and a half feet long, and kind of scratched up. There were no other dolphins around.

My sister got our dad. He drove me and the baby dolphin to Sea Life Park. We did not want to leave it in Kailua Bay because there are lots of sharks. The staff took the baby and me and put us both in the

Terry and a dolphin   Photo: Lorn Douglas

pool with their captive spinner dolphins. The whole time growing up, I only saw one other dolphin in Kailua Bay. Now I know it is very unusual for a baby to be alone.

After this experience, I did not do anything else with dolphins for almost thirty years. In 1990, I heard about someone swimming with dolphins in Waimea Bay. I went swimming every day for a month, waiting for the dolphins to come. Finally I saw them. They were a good quarter of a mile away. I dove in the water and swam out to them.

I think they were just passing through, but they turned around and came back. We began introducing ourselves. The water would go from lighter blue to darker blue, with small arrays of dolphins swimming here or there. It was magical.

I took a friend for a dolphin swim when she was seven months pregnant. We met at the beach on a beautiful sunny day. As we went out, the dolphins swam quickly by us. She could not keep up. I thought to the dolphins, "You know, she can't keep up, you guys, she's pregnant." They all gathered around her for forty-five minutes. They were either under my friend or swimming around her at the surface. I cry when they do things like that.

Dolphins love kids. When little kids come out on their boogie boards giggling and laughing, I know the dolphins are happy and playing, too.

Dolphins have an ability to tune into the energy of the person that they are with. They know the level of fear and how close to come or not to come. I see these behaviors repeatedly. My underwater camera had a flash which startled the spinner dolphins when I took pictures of

Terry and several dolphins   Photo: Lorn Douglas

them. I didn't like disturbing them, so I said, "Here is what happens when I take a picture." I sent a sunrise image, a bright light. "I will warn you when I am going to take a picture. I'll say 'Photo Op'."

Right after I gave that speech, and said, "OK, Photo Op," they were in my face! They were so close and so excited that most of the pictures were of body parts. Now when I say "Photo Op," whoever wants to be in the picture comes over, and none of them are startled anymore.

When I was a teacher, I was leaving work one day and heard a thought in my head: "You are not coming to school tomorrow, make lesson plans." It was so clear that I made lesson plans and called a substitute teacher. That night in my meditation group I heard: "Be at the beach tomorrow between eight and nine." I drove to the beach the next morning. I had never seen so many dolphins. There were at least a hundred. I ran down the trail and got in the water. There were dolphins everywhere.

Three or four of them sonared me on my chakras. I could feel it full pressure at those points, starting from the crown moving down.

Fifteen dolphins were ten feet away playing in a circle around me. They would slap their pectoral fins and I would slap my hand in response. We played peek-a-boo. Pretty soon all the dolphins joined the circle.

The intensity of their energy filled my heart. These feelings escalated and shifted me to a whole new level of being. I was in bliss for three months - nothing bothered me. Now I am learning how to live there.

One day after swimming with the dolphins, I turned around for one last look and finally got it: I am a land dolphin. I'm out here doing the dry land work. The dolphins will always be there for me. This thought eased me so much.

I see people's eyes when they come out of the water, and I feel their hearts. They have been moved by the joy dolphins share with us.

Terry and lots of dolphins   Photo: Lorn Douglas

Epilogue

The Time of the Very Beginnings

Bernard Moitessier was born in 1925 in Indo-China and much of his sailing knowledge is founded on time spent at sea with the fishermen of the Gulf of Siam. It was during this period that he acquired the feeling of communion with the sea that shaped the course of his life. In 1966, accompanied by his wife Francoise, he made one of the classic small boat voyages - 14,000 miles nonstop from the islands of the Pacific to Europe, which he describes in his book Cape Horn: The Logical Route. *Moitessier's autobiography,* Tamata and the Alliance, *was published in 1997 by Sheridan House, shortly before his death.*

The Long Way *is the story of his participation in the nonstop Round the World Race for single-handed yachts in 1968. After circling the globe ahead of his competition, Moitessier chose to drop out of the race and continue sailing halfway around the planet again without stopping, to Tahiti, where he settled rather than returning to Europe. It is a remarkable story of sailing and discovery.*

The Time of the Very Beginnings, *here in its entirety, takes place on Moitessier's passing of New Zealand.*

(Bernard Moitessier is one of my all time sailing heroes. This is the first whale tale I remember reading. -pjf)

I feel a bit washed out this morning. Not too much, though. Calms are all right. The sky has turned overcast. In any case nothing can take my Christmas night away. The wind is back, barely perceptible. More seals. 'Hello-hello.' *Joshua* glides on the flat sea at four knots due south, to give Stewart Island, 100 miles SE, as much leeway as possible. The SW tip of New Zealand is 40 miles to the east; the noon sight put it in place on the chart despite the overcast weather. You know how it is: the whole sky is covered with low clouds and you are really sure that no sight will be possible. Yet you stay on deck with the sextant ready, you follow the spots of dull light between the clouds, where the sun should be. Then you lose hope and all of a sudden boom!...here is the sun, you grab it fast and throw it on the horizon. And you get so high for the rest of the day. Got it! The wind dies. Then it comes back a little later, westerly this time, right at nightfall; very gentle, but from the west. The even rustle of water cut by the bow can be heard, on a single note as there is no pitching. I sleep, I watch, I go back to sleep, back on deck to listen to the night. All night long, I will hear the rustling of clean water cut by the bow, in the great peace of the sea and the night.

By the next noon sight, 100 miles have been covered. Stewart Island, south of New Zealand, is now 32 miles to the ENE, and the dangerous outlying reef of South Trap lies barely 44 miles due east. After that the way will be clear, with the Pacific all to myself, with only the sea and the wind as far as the Horn. For the moment though, there is no Horn. There is only Stewart Island ringed with reefs far offshore, and South Trap awash, both in the murk. From time to time, the pale disk of the sun shows through the clouds, and I was able to shoot a perfect sight at noon. The air was dry last night, there was no dew on deck, the clouds were stratus with no hidden tricks. Just some poor visibility, nothing serious.

The cloud cover thins, and what do I see but Stewart Island, right where it should be, little blue-tinted hillocks floating on the horizon to port. I am stirred to feel the Pacific so close. But the wind slackens to force 1 or 2. I continue SE to swing wide, because of the tidal currents which could carry me onto South Trap reef, just under the surface, twenty miles from Stewart. I give the island a long look. The last landmark to be seen before the Pacific. It disappears into the murk again, reappears a few minutes, hides behind a stratus. Hand-bearing compass. I feel happy.

Suddenly I notice I am starving. Landfalls are always like that. I brown four large onions in the pressure cooker, add a big piece of pork with a quart of rice and close it. The wind shifts to SW force 4, barometer steady at 1012 millibars, speed nearly seven knots. The mizzen staysail (108 sq. ft.) has been up since dawn, as well as another 86 sq. ft. staysail, making an extra 194 sq. ft. Come on *Joshua*, shake a leg! Try to leave South Trap in the wake before nightfall. Speed 7.2 knots. The bow purrs with pleasure. A delicious aroma of risotto keeps me company right to the forestay. Long live life with a good bundle of wind in the sails when the coast is near!

The sky clears as the wind freshens to force 5 from the west. Really nice weather coming back! *Joshua* tears along at 7.7 knots. Coffee, cigarette. I go on deck to watch, then below again to roll myself another cigarette and dream, listening to the water rumbling on the hull; I go up again to listen on deck, forward, aft, everywhere; I trim a sheet that is already trimmed, heave taut the staysail that is just as taut as a moment ago, but I have to heave on it again; it's like that. And the pressure cooker is getting cold; I don't give a damn, I don't have time for it. When *Joshua* has crossed the longitude of South Trap I will be able to eat and sleep, with thousands of miles of open water before the bow. But South Trap is still 23 miles to the NE.

I had a bite, all the same, and muse, sitting cross legged in front of the chart table, sipping coffee, or smoking, or glancing at the chart, or putting my head out the hatch to look forward, then at the log. No, not nervous. Just doing my job, leading *Joshua* as fast as possible along the shortest and safest path around the last pile of rock in her way at the entrance to the Pacific. In a very short time the sky has become overcast again, from one horizon to the other. But the wind is holding, the sea is still nearly calm. Its waves have not had time to build after the long rest of the last two days. One rather curious fact, for such a high latitude (nearly 48 degrees south): the very long, very high swell that usually comes from the SW or west is absent today. You would almost think it was the Mediterranean, with the *mistral* rising, but with an overcast sky.

I hear familiar whistlings and hurry out, as always when porpoises are around. I don't think I've ever seen so many at once. The water is white with their splashing, furrowed in all directions by the knives of their dorsal fins. There must be close to a hundred.

I would like to shoot some film, but it is too dark; the shots would not turn out, and I have no film to waste. An hour ago they would have given me the most beautiful pictures of the trip, with the sun all around. A tight line of 25 porpoises swimming abreast goes from stern to stem on the starboard side, in three breaths, then the whole group veers right and rushes off at right angles, all the fins cutting the water together and in the same breath taken on the fly.

I watch, wonder struck. More than ten times they repeat the same thing. Even if the sun were to return, I could not tear myself away from all this joy, all this life, to get out the Beaulieu. I have never seen such a perfect ballet. And each time, it is to the right that they rush off, whipping the sea white for thirty yards. They are obeying a precise command, that is for sure. I can't tell if it is always the same group of 20 or 25, there are too many porpoises to keep track. They seem nervous; I do not understand. The others seem nervous too, splashing along in zig-zags, beating the water with their tails, instead of playing with the bow, the way they usually do. The entire sea rings with their whistling. Another pass from stern to stem, with the same abrupt, graceful turn to the right. What are they playing at today? I have never seen this...Why are they nervous? Because they are nervous, I am sure of it. And I have never seen that, either.

Something pulls me, something pushes me. I look at the compass. *Joshua* is running downwind at 7 knots straight for Stewart Island, hidden in the stratus. The steady west wind had shifted around to the south without my realizing it. The course change was not apparent because of the quiet sea, without any swell, on which *Joshua* neither rolled nor tossed. Usually, *Joshua* always lets me know of course changes without my having to look at the compass if the sky is overcast. This time, she couldn't.

I drop the mizzen staysail, then trim the sheets and set the windvane for a beat. We are certainly more than 15 miles from the Stewart Island rocks. But since when has *Joshua* been heading for the stratus-hidden coast? Was it before the porpoises' last pass, with their right-angle turn?...Or before they showed up, even before their first demonstrations? I go below to put on my foul weather gear, as it is drizzling and there is spray now that we are close hauled. The wind has eased but not dropped, in spite of the drizzle. I wipe off my hands carefully and roll myself a cigarette, nice and dry in the cabin. I wonder about the porpoises, whose whistles I can still hear. I try to detect a difference in the loudness of the whistling. I am not sure there is any difference. It would be extraordinary if there were. But my ear is not keen enough, my auditory memory for sounds may be tricking me. If I were blind I could say for sure; the blind remember all sounds exactly. I do not know any more. It is so easy to make a mistake, and then believe anything. And to say anything at all.

I go back on deck after just a few drags on my cigarette. There are as many porpoises as before. But now they play with *Joshua*, fanned out ahead, in single file alongside, with the very lithe, very gay movements I have always known. And then something wonderful happens: a big black and white porpoise jumps ten or twelve feet in the air in a fantastic somersault, with two complete rolls. And he lands flat, tail forward. Three times he does his double roll, bursting with a tremendous joy, as if he were shouting to me and all the other porpoises: "The man understood that we were trying to tell him to sail to the right...you understood...you understood...keep on like that, it's all clear ahead!"

Standing in my foul weather gear, boots and leather gloves, I hold one of the windward mainmast shrouds. Nearly all my porpoises are now swimming on the windward side as well. That surprises me some more. Now and then they roll onto their sides, their left eyes clearly showing. I think they are looking at me. They must see me very well, thanks to the yellow foul weather gear, which stands out against the white of the sails above the red hull.

My porpoises have been swimming around *Joshua* for over two hours. The ones I have met in the past rarely stayed more than a quarter of an hour before going on their way. When they leave, all at once, two of them remain behind until twilight, a total of five full hours. They seem as if a little bored, one on the right, the other on the left. For three hours longer they swim like that, each isolated on his own side, without playing, setting their speed by *Joshua's,* two or three yards from the boat. I have never seen anything like it. Porpoises have never kept me company this long. I am sure they were given the order to stay with me until *Joshua* was absolutely out of danger. I do not watch them all the time, because I am a little worn out by the day, by the terrific tension you do not feel at the moment , when you have to give everything you've got to pass into a new ocean. I stretch out on the bunk for a little while, come up on deck, read the log, have a look around. My two porpoises are still there in the same place. I go below to mark the latest run on the chart, and lie down for a moment again. When I go on deck and climb the mast for the tenth time, to see further, my porpoises are still there, like two fairies in the waning light. I go below and close my eyes for a rest.

This is the first time that I feel such peace, a peace that has become a certainty, something that cannot be explained, like faith. I know I will succeed, and it strikes me as perfectly normal: that is the marvellous thing, that absolute certainty where there is neither pride nor fear nor surprise. The entire sea is simply singing in a way I had never known before, and it fills me with what is at once question and answer. At one point, though, I am tempted to steer for the reefs, to see what my porpoises would say. Something holds me back. When I was a little boy, my mother told me fairy tales. Once upon a time a very poor fisherman caught a big fish that had all the colours of the rainbow. And the beautiful fish begged him to spare his life. So the fisherman let him go, and the magic fish told him to make a wish any time he needed something. The fisherman asked the fish to make his thatched roof stop leaking, and could he possibly have something to eat a little less seldom. And when he went back to his hut, the roof was new, the table was set, and the soup bowl was full of lentil soup with croutons. And the poor fisherman had never been so happy, as he ate his nice hot lentil soup with croutons floating on top, in his hut with the roof that didn't leak any more. Not only that, but the bed was made, with a nice dry pallet and a brand new blanket as thick as that. But the fisherman kept asking for things, and more things, and still more things. And the more he had, the more he wanted.

Yet even when he owned a palace with lots of servants and a whole bunch of carriages in the courtyard, he was much less happy than when he used to eat his lentil soup with plenty of croutons on top, in his hut with the roof that didn't leak any more, and then used to go to sleep on his nice dry pallet, in the very first days of his friendship with the magic fish that had all the colours of the rainbow. So he asked to be the King. And at that the magic fish really got angry: he took away his friendship, and gave him back his hut with the leaky roof and the damp pallet and nothing in the soup bowl.

Marvellous things stir in my head and in my heart, as if they were about to overflow. It would be easy to slack the sheets a bit and run downwind for a few minutes toward the hidden reefs, to see what my porpoises would do. It would be easy...but the sea is still full of their friendly whistling: I can't risk spoiling what they have already given me. And I feel I am right, as one should never treat fairy tales lightly. They have taught me to understand many things, and to respect them. Thanks to Kipling's stories, I know how *Pau Amma the King Crab* invented the tides in the *Time of the Very Beginnings*, and why all crabs have pincers today, thanks to the little girl's golden scissors, and how the Elephant got his trunk from asking so many questions, and how the Leopard got those nice spots on his fur, and how maybe I will round the Horn thanks to porpoises and fairy tales, which helped me rediscover the *Time of the Very Beginnings*, where each thing is simple.

And after I plotted the last dead reckoning position on the chart, which finally put me beyond the reef, I quickly went on deck. My two porpoises were gone.

It is night. The sky has cleared, the wind is westerly again. The moon, in her first quarter, seems to hang behind the mizzen, making the sea glisten in the wake. The reef is cleared, my porpoises are gone, the way is free until the Horn. Free on the right, free on the left, free everywhere.

Taku & Lummi   *Photo: Peter Fromm*

Glossary

Whale Words:

Baleen - comblike plates in some whales' mouths which strain their food from a mouthful of water

Breach - when a cetacean jumps out of the water

Bioluminescence - plankton glowing at night when stimulated

Cetacean - the Order of whales, dolphins, and porpoises

Dorsal fin - the fin in the center of a marine animal's back

Fluke - the tail fin of a cetacean, it is horizontally oriented - fish tail fins are vertically oriented

Logging - a mode of resting on the surface with the blowhole out of the water

Pectoral fin - the side fin of a marine mammal, with similar bones as human hands.

Porpoising - when cetaceans swim fast, their bodies lunging out of the water repeatedly

Resident orca - fish-eating killer whales

Rostrum - the head, near the blowholes of a cetacean

Saddle patch - greyish-white markings below and behind the dorsal fin of an orca. They are unique, like a fingerprint

Sounding - when a cetacean dives

Spout - the exhalation of air when a cetacean surfaces

Spyhopping - when a cetacean is vertical in the water, its head in the air, so it can look around

Super pod - several pods of orcas gathered together, when they greet each other and mating occurs

Tail lobbing - slapping the water's surface with the tail

Transient orca - the marine mammal-eating killer whales

Nautical Words:

Companionway - the opening in the cabin one enters the boat through

Dinghy - a small boat, often towed behind or carried aboard a larger boat

Ketch - a sailboat with two masts, where the shorter mast is behind, and mounted ahead of the rudder post

Port side - the left hand side of the boat, when facing forward

Prop wash - the stream of water the propellor has pushed

Schooner - a sailboat with two masts, the shorter mast ahead

Sloop - a sailboat with one mast and two sails, a main and a jib

Starboard side - the right hand side of the boat, when facing forward

Steerage way - when a boat is moving through the water and the rudder will direct the boat's course

Stem - the very front part of a boat's hull

Stern - the very rear part of a boat's hull

Wind vane - a mechanical self-steering device mounted at the stern of a sailboat

Yawl - a two masted sailboat, where the shorter mast is located behind the rudder post

Acknowledgments

My sincere thanks to those people - most of them strangers - who shared their experiences with me for this second volume of Whale Tales. Their stories were tape recorded, and transcribed then mailed to them to be read for additions and corrections. I often spoke with them to get more information. Hearing the details of these interactions, and living with them through the process of making a book was wonderful. To be able to include photographs of these events is a great thrill.

This book would not be here without the dedicated assistance of Andrew Seltser and Bruce Conway, who believed in *Whale Tales* from the beginning.

Working with Andrew and Bruce included a large amount of humor and creative, constructive criticism. We spent a day riding the ferry through the islands while we arranged the stories and chapters. After completing our 'work,' we were sitting in the sun on Orcas Island waiting for the ferry to return to Friday Harbor. The man who happily agreed to take our photograph turned out to be Michael Baker - his story of communicating with a large male orca from a fourteen foot dory is in volume one! Synchronicity at its finest.

Part of the process of making Whale Tales was having people read through the unedited stories, and share their reactions to them. To Denise Acsay, Ian Byington, Susan Eyerly, and Rod Kuhlbach, I hope you can see an improvement in the finished book over what you read - I'll be in touch with stories for volume three!

My friend Doug (the Bug) Buxton, with wonderful words of wisdom, made high quality scans of the photos for the book.

Thanks also to the Silva Bay Marina & Resort for moorage while I was transcribing the stories. If you are ever on Gabriola Island, stop in and have a 'Tuna Burger.'

I deeply appreciate the support of everyone who told me they enjoyed volume one, and continually asked how the progress on volume two was going. Often, I felt like a lens, gathering the 'light' of these stories to share with others.

It has been deeply rewarding to be part of the literary world, where I have been shown more cooperation than competition - sort of like cetacean's lives.

About the Author

Peter J. Fromm has been involved with nature, environmental education and the outdoors all his life: exploring caves, climbing mountains and rocks, running rivers, ski touring, bicycle racing and touring, backpacking, sea kayaking, and sailing. He has taught many of these skills in a variety of settings, including environmental education programs and universities.

While a student at Ohio University in Athens (BFA in Photography, 1971), Peter coordinated the activities of Earth Day 1970. As a graduate student at the University of Oregon in Eugene (MS in Audio-Visual Communication

Peter in The Whale Museum   Photo: Albert Shepard

combined with Environmental Education & Recreation, 1974), Peter was active with the Outdoor Program's unique philosophy of recreation leadership, and the development of the multi-image slide show medium.

After graduating, Peter chose to learn to sail and moved to Bellingham, Washington. He has raced and cruised on more than one hundred and thirty different boats in several parts of the world. Since 1979, he has lived on *Uwila* - a custom, 1961, thirty-foot, double-ended yawl. A U.S. Coast Guard licensed Master, he has worked as Captain and naturalist on whale watching boats in the San Juan Islands since 1993.

Peter's primary profession, since 1970, has been photography, with a wide range of assignments and credits. His writing and photographs have been published in many books and magazines. He has presented his creative and inspirational multi-projector slide shows to many audiences. Peter has also had forty other kinds of jobs, from boat builder to university instructor.

Whale Tales, Human Interactions With Whales volume two is his second book.

Whale Tales Presentations

In his Whale Tales presentations, Peter Fromm engages audiences of all ages in an educational program with stories about people's encounters with whales, dolphins, and porpoises gathered from around the world. He also discusses the changing relationship between whales and humans, natural history of cetaceans, and related vocabulary.

The thirty to ninety minute Whale Tales presentation includes: story telling, historic and current slides and videos, a wide variety of marine mammal related literature, as well as questions and experiences from people present.

As a spokesperson for nature, Peter has shared Whale Tales presentations at schools, libraries, museums and community gatherings several hundred times throughout the West.

Whale Tales Testimonials

"...all students (grades 1 to 12) attended, finding an interest in both his photographic work and message." R. Spiering, Principal, Lopez School District

"The Whale Tales *presentation was informative and enlightening. The stories you shared from your book were amazing and inspiring."* C. Gilbert, Executive Director, The Whale Museum

"Your slide and lecture presentation made the evolution of our perceptions abundantly clear, providing us with plenty of food for thought about our changing relationship with the natural world." B. Kush, Marine Science Society of the Pacific Northwest

"Thank you for your excellent presentations at the Pacific Rim Whale Festival. Your commitment to public education is much appreciated." B. McIntyre, Pacific Rim National Park Reserve

---

Call For Stories

If you have had an encounter with a whale, dolphin or porpoise you would like to share for a future volume of Whale Tales, please contact Peter Fromm at Whale Tales Press. Peter will call, or meet with you, to tape record your story, then send a printout of the transcription for your additions and corrections. If we use your story, you will receive complimentary copies of the book. Photographs and videos are also welcomed for both Whale Tales books and our educational programs. Thanks!

The author urges you to learn about and support:

Natural Resources Defense Council

For 30 years, NRDC has fought to protect natural resources and ensure a safe and healthy environment. Our aggressive advocacy and influential research have cleaned up our waters, cleared the air, conserved habitat, and shielded threatened species. In the 1970s, we were instrumental in securing passage of the Clean Water Act and removing CFCs from aerosol products. In the 1990s, we spear-headed the campaign to protect Mexico's Laguna San Ignacio, the last undisturbed nursery of the gray whale—a long-fought battle that ended in victory early in 2000, when plans for a massive salt plant were abandoned. In between, NRDC lawyers and scientists won countless other victories for the environment.

NRDC is a membership organization. More than 400,000 members support our varied efforts.

Working from four offices (in New York, Washington DC, San Francisco, and Los Angeles), NRDC lawyers and scientists continue to pursue a broad range of efforts on behalf of the environment, in six broad programmatic areas:

Land and forests • Air and energy • Water and coasts
Health and the environment • Urban • Nuclear

In the United States and internationally, NRDC experts are addressing climate change, urban sprawl, and the threats posed by nuclear weapons. They are working to protect ancient forests, national parks, and ocean fisheries, to safeguard drinking water, and to reduce the use of toxic chemicals. They are tackling pollution from varied sources, from factories to tailpipes to hog farms.

For more information about NRDC, or to become a member, visit us on the web at www.nrdc.org or write to us at one of these addresses:

nrdcinfo@nrdc.org

NRDC Membership Department
40 West 20th Street
New York NY 10011

Do you know someone who loves whales?

Give them Whale Tales!

In his *Whale Tales* books, naturalist Peter J. Fromm has collected stories from folks around the world about how they met whales. These are compelling accounts of wonder, danger, excitement, and joy.

Impossible to read without being deeply touched, these stories are fascinating, modern folktales recounting deep truths in the simple words of everyday people.

To place an order for your copy of Whale Tales,
*either call **(800) 669-3950** or send this order form*
with your check or credit card information to:

Whale Tales Press, P.O. Box 865, Friday Harbor, WA 98250

Name_____

Phone (_____) _____

Address_____

City_____

State_____ Zip_____

Payment: ❏ Enclosed check/money order

            ❏ VISA_____ MasterCard_____ Expires_____

     Card #_____

     Signed_____

     __copies of Volume One @ $12.95/ea. ...._____

     __copies of Volume Two @ $13.95/ea. ...._____

     $2.05 S&H/1st book; ...._____

     $1 S&H/ea. additional book ...._____

     7.8% sales tax (if ordering in WA) ...._____

                    TOTAL enclosed ...._____